# LOOK! LOOK WHAT I CAN DO!

26

CREATIVE ACTION IDEAS
FOR UNDER SEVENS

By Kate Harrison

Editor: Brian Scott-Hughes

BBC

Designer: Tracy Carrington
Photographer: David Gee
Illustrator: Andrea Norton
Copy Editor: Dennis Ashton

*The author wishes to thank the following for their help:-*

*the staff and pupils of Holy Trinity C. of E. Primary School; the staff and children of the East Finchley Under 5's Playgroup.*

*Acknowledgment is due to the following, whose permission is required for multiple reproduction:-*

'The teddy bears' picnic' – words © 1932 B. Feldman & Co Ltd.
Reproduced by permission. EMI Music Publishing Ltd,
London WC2H 0LD.

This book is set in 11 on 13 point Helvetica Light
Typeset and printed by Ebenezer Baylis & Son Ltd
The Trinity Press, Worcester and London

Published by BBC Educational Publishing,
a division of BBC Enterprises Limited,
80 Wood Lane, London W12 0TT
© BBC Enterprises Limited 1986.
Reprinted 1990, 1992

ISBN 0 563 21218 7

# INTRODUCTION

All young children have such expressive bodies that their actions really do speak louder than words. When babies smile and reach out their hands towards the people round them, they are communicating physically. They curl their toes in contentment, kick their legs and arms in frustration or delight, and move their bodies spontaneously to rhythmic sounds.

A baby's body language is made up of signs which provoke immediate response. Few people can resist the outstretched arms and expressive eyes of a sociable six month old. From birth, babies and adults share an understanding which has a natural physical expression – a language without words.

The baby's body language develops rapidly. Two year olds stamp their feet in anger, hang their heads in shame, and jump up and down for joy. A shrug of the shoulders and a few shuffling footsteps tell us all we need to know about the mood of a stubborn seven year old. A grown-up's body, too, reveals his inner self. His thoughts and feelings show in his face, his posture, and the way he moves.

Children start life with the urge to explore their surroundings. In order to do so they have to pass a series of movement milestones – stages in physical development – which mark the acquisition of greater strength, co-ordination, and control of their bodies. These milestones are natural and inevitable. Even without help, children will eventually walk, run, and balance by themselves, but we can make the most of each movement milestone when it occurs.

'Look! Look what I can do!' will be familiar words to anyone who has daily care of under-sevens. When a child asks you to look at his latest physical achievement he is telling you that another movement milestone has been reached. At this point you can encourage his physical achievement in a number of ways.

This book deals with movement milestones in the context of creative movement and dance. It aims to provide parents, child-minders, playgroup leaders, and teachers with a guide to the physical development and creative movement potential of children from birth to seven years. It contains practical advice and many action and dance ideas which can be easily adapted to suit children of different ages, abilities, and maturity.

First come familiar rhymes, then ideas for exploring contrasting shapes and sizes. Words and rhythms are introduced as stimuli and accompaniments for actions based on everyday and imaginary activities. Many of the ideas contain enough material for several movement sessions. They can be followed literally but they are intended mainly as starting points for the children's free interpretation.

There is no single right way to introduce expressive actions to children. The ideas in this book are intended to stimulate their creative involvement, to suggest rather than dictate how they should respond. The text invites you to observe what the children do and to appreciate and applaud their efforts. It then suggests how you can introduce action ideas which will improve the children's physical abilities, encourage their development, and nurture their creative, expressive action responses. As their confidence and experience increase, they will spontaneously put forward their own ideas and develop them in their own ways.

Your observations of the children's involvement, energy, and enthusiasm will enable you to judge how much to introduce into each session. Only you can choose when to embark on new activities and how long to continue each one.

Your own enthusiasm and involvement are essential to the children's success. You can intervene to help them extend their physical skills and develop the expressive qualities of their movements. You can indicate speed and strength of actions by suggesting images: 'Creep quietly and slowly like a cat . . . pounce suddenly and strongly like a lion.' You can improve control and co-ordination by asking such questions as 'Can you reach just a little further? . . . jump a little bit higher? . . . stretch your fingers and toes more?'

As the children get older, your questions will become more challenging. You can ask them to find as many ways as they can to move in a variety of shapes and sizes, to different rhythms, inspired by all sorts of ideas.

All the suggestions in this book have been tested with many different groups of under-sevens during my years as an advisory dance teacher for children of nursery and primary school ages. They are derived from what is familiar in the home and the school. They should be approached not in isolation but as a part of daily life. They can be developed in various ways such as making models and drawing pictures. Many of the ideas have been used in BBC Education's weekly school radio series *Let's move!* (used with more than 35 000 classes) and *Time to move* (more than 26 000 classes). These programmes, broadcast on Radio 5 MW, provide a rich source of music, most of it specially commissioned and arranged specifically for young children's creative movement and dance.

# CONTENTS

# 1 INTO ACTION

LOOK! LOOK WHAT I CAN DO!

This chapter and chapters 2 and 3 outline the major movement milestones which occur from birth to seven years and suggest simple ways in which we (parents, child-minders, playgroup leaders, or nursery or infant teachers) can help the children to get the most from them. These suggestions are only a guide. Many children reach their milestones in a different order; some move rapidly from one to another, often missing out milestones on their way; others proceed at a slower pace.

## MOVEMENT MILESTONES FROM BIRTH TO ONE YEAR

The first year of life is a period of rapid growth and development. It is during this time that babies' body language develops into a form of self-expression that enables them to communicate with those around them. It is this and the need to investigate their immediate surroundings that motivate them to smile, reach out, roll over, crawl, shuffle, sit, and eventually to stand up and walk by themselves.

We can help babies to get the most from each achievement and encourage them towards their next target by enriching their physical environment and by introducing them to a variety of action rhymes and movement games which are repeatedly played with them. Suggestions are given for each group of milestones.

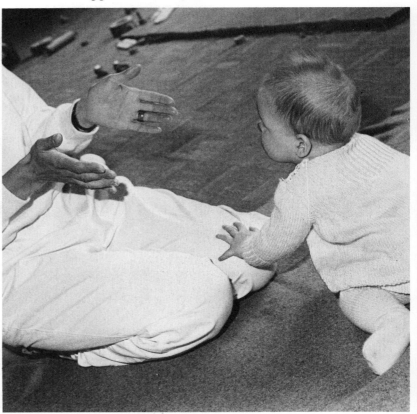

**From birth to three months**

▷ staying awake for lengthening periods
▷ becoming increasingly aware of voices and movements
▷ observing contrasts in colours and shapes
▷ starting to control the movements of the head
*Place a mirror and colourful pictures where the baby can see them. Suspend bright, sparkling mobiles from ceilings and strings of attractive shapes across his pram and cot. Put him where he can see the natural movement of trees, clouds, and birds, as well as you and others at work.*
▷ responding to the touch and attention of others
*Use every opportunity when the baby is awake and alert to talk together. Introduce and play finger and toe action games with the baby (see page 12). Rock him to the words and rhythms of suitable nursery rhymes (see page 10).*

**From three to six months**

▷ grasping and playing with fingers and toes while the baby is lying on his back
▷ lifting his head and moving around on tummy and hands
▷ wriggling and rolling first from tummy to back and, later, the other way
▷ tucking in knees and pushing hands forwards in preparation for crawling
*Encourage these early attempts at mobility by placing attractive toys all around the baby, just out of reach.*

LOOK! LOOK WHAT I CAN DO!

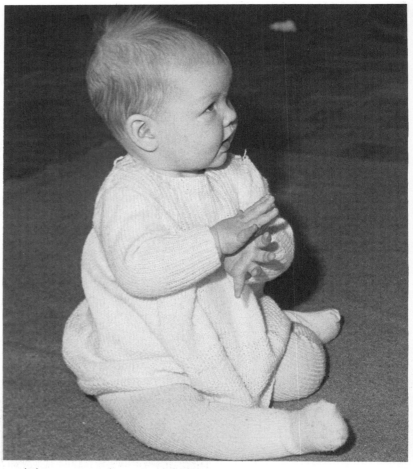

▷ sitting propped up, unaided
*Provide frequent opportunities for the baby to sit in order to develop balance and control and to allow him to observe and become more curious about his surroundings.*
▷ responding and interacting with others
*Play rhythmic rocking, jogging, and bouncing games together, holding the baby securely, using a variety of traditional rhymes (see page 10).*

**From six to eight months**  ▷ sitting upright without support, with legs wide apart
▷ co-ordinating head, eyes, hands, and arms to reach and grasp in different directions
▷ transferring objects from hand to hand
*You can help the baby to gain an awareness of shape and size by providing an assortment of attractive toys and playing appropriate action games with him (see page 12).*
▷ responding to simple, repetitive movement games
*As well as the rhymes and games the baby already knows and enjoys, introduce others, such as clapping rhymes (see page 14), to help develop co-ordination, control, and rhythm.*

**From eight to twelve months**

▷ crawling on hands and knees or creeping on hands and feet
*Provide push-along toys to encourage mobility.*
▷ becoming absorbed in play for lengthening periods
▷ increasing control of hands and fingers
*Introduce toys which can be taken apart and reassembled, and which require shapes and sizes to be matched and sorted.*
▷ initiating play with adults and siblings
*Add to the baby's developing repertoire of nursery rhymes and songs and action games as well as repeating favourites. Be sure to show how much you appreciate and are amused by his efforts since reinforcement at every milestone builds confidence and competence.*

## MOVEMENT MILESTONES FROM ONE TO TWO YEARS

In the second year of life, babies become bigger and stronger, more independent, inquisitive, imaginative, and adventurous. Their first tentative steps mark the beginning of their physical freedom to explore and investigate their surroundings.

This delightful but difficult age needs constant supervision, and we must make sure that toddlers have a safe, secure environment in which to play. Physical freedom and creative, constructive play at this stage of their development paves the way towards greater confidence and control.

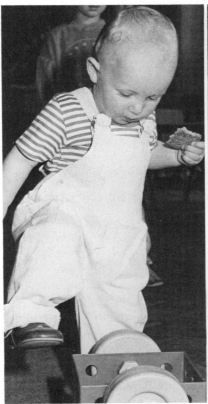
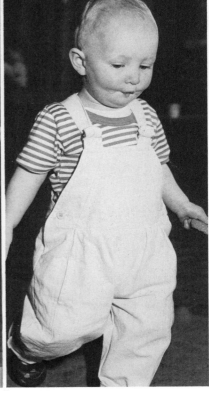

**From twelve to eighteen months**

▷ crawling rapidly
▷ pulling themselves up to stand and falling backwards to sit
▷ walking unaided with feet apart and hands held high
*Provide an uncluttered floorspace in which these developing skills can be practised and offer praise and encouragement at each new achievement. Make the most of the baby's spontaneous falls by playing bouncing and falling rhymes (see page 12).*
▷ balancing and bending to pick up objects
*Play stretching and bending games to help develop balance and control (see page 16).*
▷ sleeping for shorter periods each day
*Continue to induce periods of rest or quiet with rhythmic, rocking rhymes (see page 10).*

**From eighteen months to two years**

▷ climbing up and down stairs, under and over furniture, in order to explore the immediate environment
*Supervise the toddler's activities and anticipate dangers; for example, erect safety gates at the tops and bottoms of staircases. Instead of disposing of large cardboard boxes, use them for clambering into, over, between, and around.*
▷ attempting to jump from two feet to two feet
*Hold the child's hands and lift him off the ground each time he lifts his shoulders. This will introduce the sense of elevation.*
▷ walking confidently with feet closer together
*Give every opportunity to practise this developing skill by going for frequent walks to places of interest such as parks, playgrounds, and supermarkets. Always take a pushchair with you.*
▷ imitating everyday activities such as sweeping, polishing, hammering, and digging.
*Provide a number of safe everyday household utensils (a spoon, a saucepan) and toy versions of adult implements (a tool kit, a broom) so that the child can imitate your working actions and those of others. Reinforce them by saying and playing together appropriate repetitive action rhymes.*
▷ jigging and jogging to rhythmic sounds
*Introduce and play frequently a wide selection of music and songs, on tape or record, which invite and encourage spontaneous, uninhibited movement responses.*

## MOVEMENT MILESTONES FROM TWO TO THREE YEARS

The third year of life is a year of changes and challenges, tempers and tantrums. It is an active, inquisitive, boisterous, and mischievous phase which is hard to contain within the boundaries of the home. Two to three year olds are constantly on the move and need new outlets for their physical and emotional energies. It is during this year that the toddler evolves into a playful pre-school child.

Each movement milestone now becomes a game in itself as, with increasing confidence, the children explore all sorts of new ways to tiptoe, step, run, and jump from one milestone to the next. Almost daily, new milestones are conquered and controlled and, although physical growth begins to slow down, there is rapid progress in the acquisition of mental and muscular skills.

▷ walking confidently alone

*Whenever possible, resist the temptation to use the pushchair or car for short journeys. Try instead to provide frequent opportunities for the child to discover the joy of walking confidently unaided.*

▷ clambering with increasing skill and confidence up, over, through, and around large objects

▷ gradually gaining control of whole-body actions such as running, jumping, balancing, throwing, and kicking

*Visit parks and safe open spaces where the youngster can walk, run, clamber, and climb freely. If possible, introduce a few large pieces of apparatus into your home (there are several climbing frames available which can be altered and added to as the child grows up), erecting them on a safe surface (grass, not concrete) and keeping them low until skill, confidence, and control have developed. Until then, supervision is essential. However, do not be over-protective; most children know their limitations and will not attempt something they cannot achieve.*

▷ running and stopping with increasing control

*Play going-and-stopping games together such as musical bumps (stopping with the music and falling to the floor) and later, as control is established, musical statues (stopping and freezing in a standing position).*

▷ growing and shrinking into different whole-body shapes

*Play games which will encourage moving slowly and quickly into a variety of body shapes (see page 16). Repeat them frequently, and help improve the actions by suggesting 'stretch just a little bit taller' or 'reach to the very ends of your fingertips'.*

▷ balancing on tiptoe for a few seconds

▷ tiptoeing slowly

*Once he can tiptoe slowly, the child has gained whole-body control. Give plenty of practice.*

▷ jumping from two feet to two feet

*At the beginning of their third year, children often express a jump by simply shrugging their shoulders, without taking their feet from the ground. Gradually, with the help of jumping games and action rhymes, their jumps will gain elevation and they will begin to bounce.*

▷ pushing, lifting, and pulling large objects from one place to another

▷ constructing with increasing imagination

*Extend the youngsters' creative play by providing large cardboard boxes which they can transform into trains, cars, houses, and so on.*

▷ gaining finer finger control

*Play finger rhymes which will give the children opportunities to explore the possibilities of all sorts of hand and finger shapes and actions (see page 12).*

▷ playing for short periods with other children

*It now becomes increasingly important to provide social opportunities for the children to play alongside others of a similar age. Invite one or two playmates to your home or join a parent and toddler group which will enable you to share supervision and responsibility. Use these occasions to introduce simple movement games which will encourage the children to play together. Many of the action ideas in this book can be easily adapted.*

▷ enjoying all sorts of physically creative play pursuits

*Many sports centres provide a baby gymnasium which allows two to three year olds to explore different pieces of large, safe apparatus designed specifically to meet their needs. If your local sports centre has such a facility, use it frequently.*

▷ resting for shorter periods in the day

*Continue to encourage quiet times, as and when they are needed, using favourite rocking rhymes and songs (see page 10).*

▷ inventing imaginary playmates

*Erect a tent or playhouse into which the youngster can retreat from time to time. Do not intervene in this private world unless you are invited, as it is during this period that children enter the world of make-believe.*

▷ demanding constant attention and appreciation
*Be ready to stop and look at what your child can do. Remember, each milestone needs your encouragement, praise, and reinforcement.*
▷ using whole-body actions in inventive and imaginative ways to express words and music
▷ participating co-operatively with others in dancing and movement games
*Whenever friends come to play, organise movement and dancing games. Many ideas will be found throughout this book.*

## ACTION IDEAS FOR UNDER-THREES

Babies take pleasure in the rhythm and sound of words and music long before they have command of speech or can fully understand the spoken word. They are active, responsive, rhythmic individuals who, from the start, need challenging, stimulating outlets for their developing physical and creative abilities. By providing such opportunities, we are increasing the confidence and control with which they will progress towards future movement milestones.

Most of us provide these opportunities instinctively and spontaneously by passing on to our children the action games and nursery rhymes and songs we learnt in our own childhood. Their simplicity, rhythm, and humour give them an everlasting appeal and they provide ideal stimuli for creative movement activities for the very young, who express their imaginations in a largely physical way.

Very young children need a simple, structured approach to movement. All the following rhymes have clear rhythms to which they can react spontaneously.

## Rocking rhymes

Introduce rocking rhymes from a very young age, holding the baby close and rocking together to the rhythm of the words or melody. When he can sit without support, put him on your knee, hold both his hands securely, and rock gently together forwards and backwards and from side to side. The rhymes can also be used to encourage rest or sleep.

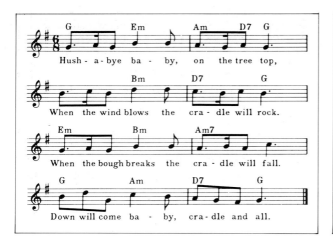

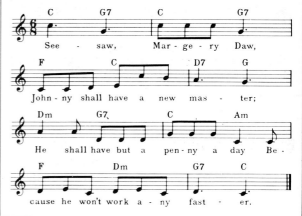

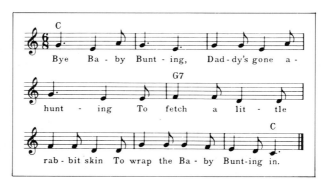

These rhymes also have slow, gentle, rocking rhythms.

We'll sit by the fire
And I'll give her some food,
And she will love me
If I'm gentle and good.

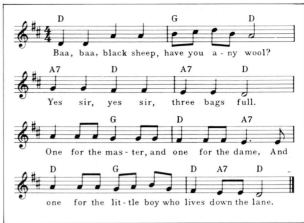

## Bouncing rhymes

Sit baby on your knee holding his waist or, once he can sit unaided, both hands. Bounce up and down together to the rhythm of the words or music.

Trot, trot, trot,
Go and never stop.
Trudge along, my little pony,
Where 'tis rough and where 'tis stony.
Go and never stop,
Trot, trot, trot, trot, trot!

To market, to market, to buy a fat pig;
Home again, home again, jiggety jig.
To market, to market, to buy a fat hog;
Home again, home again, jiggety jog.

The lady went to market, clip, clip, clop.
The gentleman went to market, trot, trot, trot.
But when the farmer went to market,
He went gallop-a-gallop-a-gallop
All the way there!

Ten galloping horses came to town,
Five were white, and five were brown.
They galloped up, they galloped down,
And then they galloped right out of town.

LOOK! LOOK WHAT I CAN DO!

## Bouncing and falling rhymes

Bounce together rhythmically. Then, holding the baby firmly, open your knees on the appropriate word so that he drops between them almost to the floor. Later, as the baby develops, he can jig and jog rhythmically while standing and then fall all the way to the floor by himself.

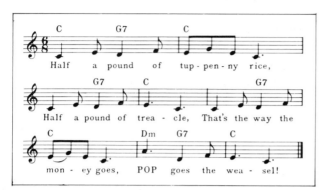

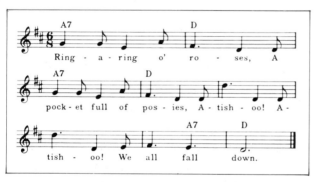

Father and Mother and Big Brother John
Went to market one by one.
Father fell off!
Mother fell off!
But Big Brother John went on and on
And on and on and on.

## Finger and toe rhymes

Here is the church
*Touch fists at knuckles.*
Here is the steeple
*Open fists and touch fingertips.*
Open the doors
*Open hands wide.*
And here are the people.
*Wriggle fingers*
Here is the parson going upstairs
*Walk fingers upwards into the air.*
And here he is a-saying his prayers.
*Put hands together as for prayer.*

Slowly, slowly, very slowly
Creeps the garden snail.
Slowly, slowly, very slowly
Up the wooden rail.

Quickly, quickly, very quickly
Runs the little mouse.
Quickly, quickly, very quickly
Round about the house.

*Tiptoe and run fingers up and down
baby's arm or leg; finish each verse
with a tickle.*

Incy Wincy spider
Climbed up the water spout
*Tiptoe fingers up into the air.*
Down came the raindrops
And washed poor Incy out.
*Flutter fingers down again.*
Out came the sunshine
And dried up all the rain
*Stretch arms wide.*
And Incy Wincy spider
Climbed up the spout again.
*Tiptoe fingers high in the air.*

*Later this rhyme can be used for
whole-body actions (see page 17).*

I had a little brother
No bigger than my thumb
*Hold up a thumb.*
I put him in the coffee pot
*Put thumb into fist of other hand
(or baby's fist).*
He rattled like drum!
*Wriggle finger about.*

Walking round the garden
Like a teddy bear
*Use a finger to draw circles on the palm of baby's hand.*
One step, two steps,
*Tiptoe your fingers up baby's arm.*
Tickly under there!
*Finish with a surprise tickle in a ticklish spot.*

Knock, knock at the door
*Make knocking actions with fists.*
Pull, pull down the bell
*Reach high with both arms and pull hands down.*
Peep, peep through the keyhole
*Join first finger and thumb into a keyhole shape.*
Turn, turn the handle
*Make turning actions with hands.*
And walk right in.
*Tiptoe fingers in the air.*

Two little dickie birds sitting on a wall
*Form beak shapes with both hands using
first fingers and thumbs.*
One named Peter, one named Paul.
*Open and close each beak in turn.*
Fly away, Peter! Fly away, Paul!
*Flutter each hand out of sight behind back.*
Come back, Peter! Come back, Paul!
*Flutter each hand back again.*

This little pig went to market,
This little pig stayed at home;
This little pig had roast beef,
This little pig had none.
And this little pig cried 'Wee-wee-wee'
All the way home!

*Tweak each toe (or finger) in turn starting from the
big toe (or thumb); finish by running your finger up
baby's leg (or arm).*

*Hold and wiggle both baby's big toes (or thumbs),
leaving go of each in turn on 'pop' and 'bang';
repeat the actions holding each pair of toes (or
fingers) in turn, reducing the number of sausages
each time (8, 6, 4, 2).*

## Clapping and stamping rhymes

Rain, rain, go away,
Come again another day.
Rain, rain, go away,
Come again on washing day.

Pat-a-cake pat-a-cake,
Baker's man,
Bake me a cake
As fast as you can.
Pat it and prick it
And mark it with B,
And put it in the oven
For Baby and me.

**Dancing rhymes**     Introduce recordings of favourite nursery rhymes and other popular songs for the children to respond to freely. Make dancing very much part of their everyday life. All toddlers will dance spontaneously when a familiar, favourite piece of music is played.

Sing a song of six-pence, a pock-et-ful of rye.
Four and twen-ty black-birds baked in a pie.
When the pie was o-pened the birds be-gan to sing. Now
was-n't that a dain-ty dish to set be-fore the King.

Hey did-dle did-dle, the cat and the fid-dle, The
cow jumped o - ver the moon. The
lit - tle dog laughed to see such fun, And the
dish ran a - way with the spoon.

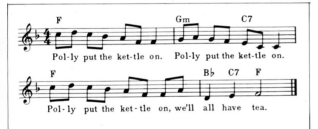

Pol-ly put the ket-tle on. Pol-ly put the ket-tle on.
Pol-ly put the ket-tle on, we'll all have tea.

Here we go Loo - by Loo,
Here we go Loo - by Light,
Here we go Loo - by Loo,
All on a Sat - ur - day night.

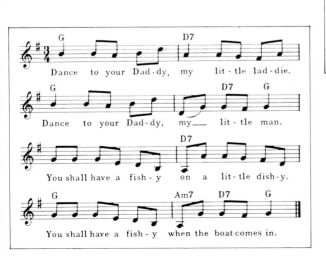

Dance to your Dad-dy, my lit - tle lad-die.
Dance to your Dad-dy, my lit - tle man.
You shall have a fish - y on a lit - tle dish-y.
You shall have a fish - y when the boat comes in.

## Whole-body action rhymes

Hands clap,
Fingers wriggle,
Arms wave,
Thumbs wiggle,
Toes waggle,
Heels thump,
Legs run,
Feet jump.
*Accompany each line with*
*the appropriate action.*

I'm as small as a mouse
*Curl up small with knees on the*
*floor and head and elbows tucked*
*away.*
As tall as a house
*Slowly grow tall with fingertips*
*leadings.*
As wide as a gate
*Stretch arms wide and stand with*
*legs wide apart.*
And as thin as a pin
*Drop arms at sides and pull in*
*tummy and cheeks.*

*Once the rhyme is familiar, change*
*the order of the lines so that the*
*children listen, then move. Also,*
*say the lines sometimes slowly*
*and sometimes quickly in order to*
*change the speed of their actions.*

Mix a pancake,
Stir a pancake,
Pop it in the pan.
Fry the pancake,
Toss the pancake,
Catch it if you can!
*Accompany the words with stirring,*
*throwing, catching, and jumping*
*actions.*

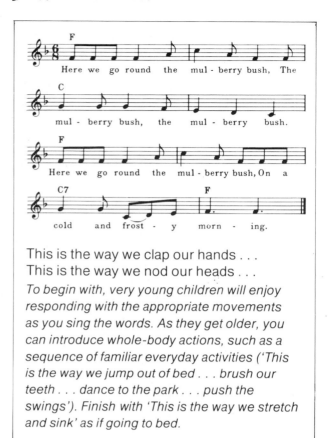

Here we go round the mul-berry bush, The mul-berry bush, the mul-berry bush. Here we go round the mul-berry bush, On a cold and frost-y morn-ing.

This is the way we clap our hands . . .
This is the way we nod our heads . . .
*To begin with, very young children will enjoy*
*responding with the appropriate movements*
*as you sing the words. As they get older, you*
*can introduce whole-body actions, such as a*
*sequence of familiar everyday activities ('This*
*is the way we jump out of bed . . . brush our*
*teeth . . . dance to the park . . . push the*
*swings'). Finish with 'This is the way we stretch*
*and sink' as if going to bed.*

I'm a little teapot, short and stout
*Stand with feet a little way apart and arms stretched wide.*
Here's my handle, here's my spout
*Bend elbow and place one hand on hip and stretch the other*
*arm to the side, above shoulder height.*
When I see the teacups, hear me shout
*Shrug shoulders on 'shout'.*
'Tip me up and pour me out!'
*Tilt sideways, first towards the bent elbow and then*
*towards the outstretched arm.*

Stretch and grow, reach up high;
Stand on tip-i-toes, touch the sky!
Shrink down low, down to the floor;
Now no one can see you any more!
*Start and finish in a low, curled position with knees on the*
*floor and head and elbows tucked away. Remember to*
*pretend the youngster can no longer be seen.*

Something very special happens towards the end of the third year. Slowly but surely, the children begin to use their whole bodies rather than only their fingers and arms to express action and nursery rhymes. For example, whereas they had previously used only their fingers and arms to show Incy Wincy spider climbing up the water spout, they can now, with guidance, make their whole bodies spidery.

Incy Wincy spider
*Slowly uncurl and stretch on to hands and feet from small, round shapes into wide, spindly, balanced ones.*
Climbed up the water spout
*Step silently on hands and feet, finishing in a wide, spindly shape.*
Down came the rain
*A sudden, curling action with tucked away knees, arms, and head.*
And washed poor Incy out
*Roll gently from side to side.*
Out came the sunshine
*Slowly rise and stretch into wide, stretched, standing shapes with long necks and with faces looking upwards.*
And dried up all the rain
*Dance from place to place with legs wide apart and arms outstretched.*
So Incy Wincy spider
*Wide, stretched shapes as before on hands and feet.*
Climbed up the spout again.
*Scurry quickly and lightly from place to place, finishing with a wide, stretched balance.*

# 2 READY...STEADY ...GO!

## MOVEMENT MILESTONES FROM THREE TO FIVE YEARS

Three to five year olds are physical, imaginative individuals who need frequent interaction with other children of a similar age. They will benefit greatly from joining a playgroup or nursery class where, in a friendly and uninhibited atmosphere, they can channel their physical and creative energies into satisfying play pursuits and acquire greater emotional and social control.

In children's make-believe world, their bodies can be and do almost anything. Watch how they play imaginative games together and you will see how much they rely on movement as a means of communication and expression. You may see games of goodies and baddies, in which they run, dodge, and dart from space to space, and games of mums and dads, in which they imitate our everyday working actions, rhythmically sweeping, stirring, and hammering with enthusiasm and energy. Words may also be involved, but movement is always the main means of expression and communication.

Spurred on by the example of others, the children now become increasingly confident and adventurous in what they do. Established movement skills are performed with greater co-ordination and control and new milestones are mastered almost every day.

**From three to four years ·**
▷ running and stopping with increasing control
▷ jumping with increasing elevation
▷ balancing on one foot
▷ hopping from foot to foot and, for longer periods, on one foot without loss of balance
▷ moving in contrasting ways, such as tiptoeing and marching, striding and creeping, crawling and galloping
▷ shrinking and growing into different shapes and sizes
▷ rolling sideways while curled up small
▷ playing co-operatively with others
▷ dressing up and creating make-believe characters
▷ dancing to rhythmic sounds and music

**From four to five years**
▷ stepping, galloping, trotting, and skipping rhythmically
▷ balancing on different parts of the body with increasing control; for example, on one hand and two feet
▷ walking and jumping backwards
▷ rolling head over heels
▷ using large apparatus with increasing confidence and imagination
▷ moving with others in circles and lines
▷ moving at contrasting speeds (quickly and slowly) and strengths (strongly and lightly)

As their movement skills develop and they learn to co-operate with others and can concentrate on one activity for increasingly longer periods, pre-school children need new outlets for their physical and creative energies. It is now that we should being to structure specific movement sessions which will not only allow the children to have fun while expressing themselves in a physical way, but also prepare them for the more challenging movement and dance lessons which will eventually become part of their infant school routine.

READY . . . STEADY . . .

**What to wear**

Nursery and playgroups often take place in old buildings so check the floor for loose floorboards and splinters and then decide whether or not the children can move barefooted. All shoes restrict the expressive nature of movement; children should be able to feel the floor with their bare feet and stretch and flex their toes. If footwear must be worn, soft-soled shoes are essential. Never allow the children to wear heavy shoes, nor just socks or tights, since these can cause accidents on slippery surfaces.

Encourage the children to take off as much clothing as possible. Ideally they should be stripped down to vests and pants. As you will be required to join in the action from time to time, make sure that you are appropriately dressed. Movement is hard, hot work and too many clothes restrict whole-body expressions.

**How much space?**

The minimum amount of space you will require for your movement sessions will allow the children to stretch their arms wide and turn around on the spot without touching anyone else. If your play area is too small, divide the group and hold separate sessions. Ideally, the children should be able to move about freely without colliding. If the room is very big you may want to make a barrier of chairs to limit the size of the movement area, otherwise your voice and the children could get lost. Whatever space you have, make sure that it is free of any obstructions and that potential sources of danger such as pillars are well protected.

**Rhythmic accompaniments**

At times you will need a tambourine or small drum. This will enable you to control the children's actions by suggesting the speed and rhythm of their movements and indicating when they should start and stop. If you wish to use recorded music, you will need a record or cassette player too. Make sure there is a power point and that your machine is loud enough to fill the movement area.

**Planning the session**

Finally, you must think about what you wish the children to do. At this stage it is not enough simply to occupy them with action rhymes and games they already know. Their developing minds and bodies require the constant challenge of new, exciting action ideas and movement opportunities. Some suggestions can be found at the end of this chapter.

Each movement session should fall into four sections:
▷ an introductory group activity to establish concentration
▷ familiar action ideas which recall and develop movement material from previous sessions
▷ new action ideas which allow the children to create and explore in different ways
▷ a final group activity which brings the children together again and quietens them down

**Your role**

Remember that young children are very sensitive to the attitudes and involvement of adults. Your energy, enthusiasm, and participation are essential to the success of your movement sessions. You must be ready to take part in the activities yourself, not only by encouraging and commenting on the children's movement, but also by joining in. You will sometimes need to illustrate or clarify an action and to become part of group activities. The extent of your active participation depends on your observations of the children's needs. Every group is unique and only you can judge when to take part and when to stand back to allow the children creative freedom. Observation and a positive, enthusiastic approach are the keys to a successful and enjoyable session.

**Use of language**

From the start, it is important to be aware of the language you use to generate the children's responses. Action words alone are not always enough; descriptive words and evocative images colour the children's imaginations and encourage greater effort and achievement. They will respond more creatively and expressively if asked to 'tiptoe with long, silent steps like a prowling cat . . . stamp with heavy feet like an angry giant . . . trot lightly with high knees like a proud pony . . .'

**Session duration**

The duration of your movement sessions will be determined by the children's age, energy, enthusiasm, and involvement. Their responses and concentration will indicate when they have had enough for that day. Start with short sessions of not more than ten or fifteen minutes and, as the children mature and develop, gradually build up to half an hour or so. It is always better to leave them wanting more rather than bored and lifeless.

...GO!

*The following action ideas are presented in sequence as an illustration of how your first few movement sessions might be structured.*

**Into the movement space**    Before you go together into your movement space, ask the children to form a follow-my-leader line behind you. Then, accompanying the action with a gentle, rhythmic tap or clap, lead them slowly on tiptoe into the movement area and settle down together quietly in a corner.

**A simple starter**    A calm, controlled atmosphere at the start of the session is crucial to its success. If the children are boisterous and over-excited they will neither listen nor concentrate; chaos can ensue. Begin as a group with a popular, familiar action rhyme which you can perform together while seated, using hands and arms only, in order to gain the children's complete attention and immediate involvement.

**Finding a space**    When all eyes and ears are firmly attentive, it is time for you and the children to make your first move together by tiptoeing slowly and silently into open spaces. Begin by rising up high on tiptoe. Then, accompanied by a gentle, rhythmic beat or clap, practise tiptoeing away from each other and back together to form a secure group again. Ask the children to stay very still in their spaces and tiptoe among them, praising their efforts. Alternatively, ask them to check they have enough space round them by stretching out their arms sideways and turning on the spot.

This simple spacing game can be extended in later sessions to include other travelling actions (such as striding, marching, trotting, running, hopping, and dancing) which will allow you to repeat the activity frequently without losing the children's interest.

It is difficult for young children to grasp the idea of the need for sufficient space in which to move freely. They bunch together spontaneously and you will find that frequent practice and constant reminders are necessary.

**From space to space**

Having practised moving into spaces, the children are now ready to practise moving from space to space without colliding. Tiptoe statues (a simpler version of musical statues) provides the perfect introduction. Ask the children to tiptoe in and out of each other 'slowly and without touching anyone else at all' and, each time you clap your hands, to freeze and stay as still as they can. There are no winners (and certainly no losers) but those with quick reactions or skilful body management should be praised for their achievements.

**Statue shapes**

After a few statue stops suggest stopping in statue shapes which will challenge the children's imaginations and encourage them to use their bodies in different ways. Again the language you use will greatly improve their efforts. Write down a few words and images before the session so that you will not be lost for ideas, and be sure to include opportunities to make statues of contrasting shapes and sizes. Compare a stretched, wide shape like a wall with a tall, thin shape like a rocket; a low, round shape like a snowball with a twisted spiral like a helter-skelter.

**Moving statues**

Statue shapes can be the starting point for any creative movement activity. Once the children have had a chance to explore several ideas, add to their enjoyment of the game and to their movement skills by suggesting that they bring their statue shapes to life. Allow them to develop their own ideas at first and then suggest other creations that will extend their actions – 'jumping with legs wide apart like a bouncing bear . . . galloping with high knees like a cowboy . . . dancing spikily like an ugly witch.'

**Spacing**

The children's natural tendency at this age is to move in ever-decreasing circles. You will need to give them constant reminders to move 'this way and that . . . in and out . . . from space to space . . .' Encourage them to hold their body shapes for a few silent seconds before moving, to start only when you signal them to do so, and to freeze in their original shapes when you signal them to stop.

Before the children tire of this activity, bring them together once more as a group by asking them to tiptoe their final statue shape – 'slowly and without touching anyone else at all' – back to you. Spend a moment or two talking about some of their shape creations and actions, then suggest a group activity which you can play together. Action ideas are given later in this chapter.

**Appreciation**

Praise all the children's achievements and ask those with original ideas to demonstrate their statue shapes so that others will see what is expected of them. If any of the children are reluctant to join in any of the activities, do not force them to do so or give excessive encouragement. They will take part when they are ready, even if it is several sessions later.

**A quiet ending**

In order to finish your first movement session in the quiet, controlled way in which it began, ask the children to tiptoe into spaces of their own and curl up as small as they can. Tell them that you are going to touch them gently one by one and, when they are touched, they must stand without a sound and tiptoe along behind you, as before, in a follow-my-leader line. Emphasise that only the stillest children will be selected and that, as they are touched, they join the end of the line. When the line is complete, finish the session by leading the children out of the movement area.

LOOK! LOOK WHAT I CAN DO!

## ACTION IDEAS FOR THREES TO FIVES

The following games can be repeated from session to session with sustained enjoyment. Many other action ideas throughout the book can be easily and creatively explored and adapted for use with this age group.

## CIRCLE GAMES

All circle games should begin with the children holding hands to ensure good spacing. Arms should be slightly raised but not fully stretched, and it is important to establish the 'no pulling' rule from the start. Begin by walking round and round together while still holding hands, ensuring that the circle remains wide and the children well spaced.

It may be some time before the children can form a group circle quickly and efficiently and stay in their places as the circle moves, but with practice and repetition they will learn to do so with the minimum of help and guidance.

**What's the time, Mr Wolf?**    What's the time, Mr Wolf? is an appealing game giving excellent circle-making practice. From their places around the circle, the children tiptoe towards you (in the centre of the room) with big, slow, silent steps as they quietly ask together 'What's the time, Mr Wolf?' At the end of the phrase, they freeze until you suddenly reply 'It's breakfast (play, lunch, tea, or supper) time', when they run quickly back to their original places. (A version of this game for older children is described on page 119.)

**The farmer's in his den**

The farmer needs a wife . . .
The wife needs a . . .

Stand in the centre of the children's circle in the role of the farmer. Indicate the direction in which the children should dance as they sing the rhyme together. At the end of the first verse, invite a child into the centre of the circle to be your wife. That child then chooses another child to be a dog, cat, horse, or any other animal. Subsequent children choose different animals. As each animal companion is chosen, that child joins the group inside the circle.

The game can be developed so that, as each new animal is named, but before a new companion is chosen, the children in the circle make appropriate statue shapes.

**Circle statues**

Circle statues, a variation of musical statues, will help the children to control and maintain their circle shape. To begin with, you must stand in the centre of the circle, with your eyes closed and tapping your tambourine rhythmically, while the children tiptoe slowly and silently round and round. Each time you stop tapping and open your eyes, the children freeze in statue shapes (their own or shapes which you suggest) in their places around the circle.

**Here we go round the mulberry bush**

In 'Here we go round the mulberry bush', join the children's circle and dance round with them each time you sing the chorus together. For each verse, the circle stops and everyone performs the appropriate actions on the spot. Be ready to suggest a variety of possibilities, although the children will offer their own ideas once they are familiar with the game.

**Follow-my-leader**

Follow-my-leader is an excellent way of improving and extending the children's movement abilities and can be played with only two or with a large group. Organise the children into a line, with yourself as leader (although very soon the children will want to lead the line themselves), emphasising the importance of staying in line. This helps to establish 'no overtaking' as the golden rule of all follow-my-leader activities.

Lead the line with different actions all over the movement area, accompanying each action with appropriate rhythmic taps or shakes of your drum or tambourine. Progress from a slow, controlled action to more vigorous and faster actions such as striding, stamping, and hopping. Then enjoy transforming the line into a fairground train (shuffling round and round with turning-elbow wheels), a giant centipede (with quiet tiptoe feet, stretched arms and wriggling fingers), and a mighty monster (plodding along on wide feet with sharp, stretched claws). The movement possibilities of a follow-my-leader line are virtually unlimited.

## NURSERY RHYME GAMES

Nursery rhymes are full of physical fun and provide excellent opportunities for the children to practise and perfect all their newly acquired body skills in an enjoyable, exciting, creative way. Each rhyme can be taught in one movement session; practise the individual actions first and then combine them in sequence to show the rhyme in movement all the way through. Just as action games can be repeated and enjoyed over and over again, so nursery rhyme sequences can be improved on time after time.

**Wee Willie Winkie**

Wee Willie Winkie
Runs through the town,
Upstairs and downstairs
In his nightgown;
Tapping at the window,
Crying through the lock,
'Are all the children in their beds?
For now it's eight o'clock!'

Begin by running all over the movement space, making sudden statue stops in high and stretched or low and crouched shapes. A rhythmic beat accompanies high and low tapping actions. Then yawn and slowly stretch into wide, still, statue shapes. To finish, the children sink to the floor one by one and curl up small when you touch them to suggest putting them to bed.

## Little Miss Muffet

Little Miss Muffet
Sat on her tuffet,
Eating her curds and whey;
There came a big spider,
Who sat down beside her
And frightened Miss Muffet away.

Start with the children seated and making exaggerated scooping and eating actions in time to a slow, steady, rhythmic drumbeat or to the words of the rhyme. Next they quickly curl up small and then slowly uncurl and stretch on to hands and feet in still, balanced, spidery shapes. To finish the rhyme, they can either scurry quickly and quietly on hands and feet as the spider, or run this way and that on tiptoe as Little Miss Muffet.

## Twinkle, twinkle, little star

Twinkle, twinkle, little star,
How I wonder what you are;
Up above the world so high,
Like a diamond in the sky.
Twinkle, twinkle, little star,
How I wonder what you are.

From low, curled positions, the children make sudden jerky actions with their fingers, then their elbows and heads, after which they jump up on to two wide-spaced feet and form star shapes. Next they make light, bouncing jumps on wide-spaced feet with fingers, knees, and elbows shooting high and low in the air. They freeze in a final high, stretched shape and end the sequence by turning and sinking slowly and gently into a low, curled position.

## Jack be nimble

Jack be nimble,
Jack be quick,
Jack jump over the candlestick!

Play short, quick, tapping phrases on a drum or tambourine to which the children run and freeze. Then play slower, stronger rhythmic beats to which they leap high in the air.

## The grand old Duke of York

The grand old Duke of York,
He had ten thousand men,
He marched them up to the top of the hill,
And he marched them down again.
And when they were up, they were up,
And when they were down, they were down,
And when they were only half way up,
They were neither up nor down.

Repeat the rhyme several times, clapping the marching beat together. Then play a marching drumbeat and practise marching about with swinging arms and rhythmic steps. Introduce the idea of stopping and saluting each time the drumbeat stops. Practise growing and shrinking into a variety of high and low statue shapes before playing a marching and stopping game in which the children make appropriate high or low shapes on the words 'up' and 'down'. A follow-my-leader line will increase enjoyment.

**Hey diddle diddle!**

Hey diddle diddle!
The cat and the fiddle,
The cow jumped over the moon.
The little dog laughed to see such fun,
And the dish ran away with the spoon.

First, the children stretch slowly from low, curled shapes into long, stretched cat shapes on hands and feet. They then creep like cats, pounce to represent the cow jumping over the moon, and finish by dancing in pairs as the dish and the spoon, either holding each other by both hands and dancing round on the spot or holding one hand and dancing round and round the room.

**Humpty Dumpty**

Humpty Dumpty sat on a wall,
Humpty Dumpty had a great fall,
All the king's horses
And all the king's men
Couldn't put Humpty together again.

Chant the rhyme together several times to establish a gentle, slow, rocking rhythm. Then, from being curled up small, the children grow upwards slowly and smoothly into wide shapes with outstretched arms, pushed-out tummies, and puffed-out cheeks. Recite the rhyme as before while the children rock rhythmically from side to side in their Humpty Dumpty shapes, collapsing to the floor on the word 'fall'. Practise sudden, jerky actions using fingers, toes, elbows, and knees to make jagged, broken eggshell shapes on the floor, then gallop round and round in big circles as horses with heads high and knees and elbows raised, and march straight and tall like soldiers. Finish the rhyme by jumping into a standing jagged, broken eggshell shape and, after freezing for a moment, sink slowly and sadly down to the floor.

**Old MacDonald's farm**

Old MacDonald had a farm
Ee aye ee aye oh
And on that farm he had some . . .

Before introducing the animals (which offer opportunities to create a wide range of exciting shapes and travelling actions) work on the farmer pulling on imaginary wellington boots, striding about, stamping on the spot with high knees and strong, flat feet.

**Hens**

From curled positions wriggle up into hen shapes on wide-apart, bent legs with pushed-out tummies and bent elbow wings. Practise in turn nodding heads rhythmically, ruffling feathers, and wiggling tails. Scurry quickly and quietly this way and that on wide-apart feet and without loss of body shape. Introduce stopping in spaces to nod and peck, to shake feathery elbow wings or to wiggle feathery tails.

**Cats**

Start curled up small on hands and knees and slowly uncurl and stretch on to hands and feet. Practise creeping slowly with stretched, silent steps. Introduce pauses in which the children lift and arch their backs. Practise other cat-like actions such as pouncing, rolling, and balancing on tiptoe, with the emphasis always on control and quiet.

**Rabbits**

At first, jump in low, crouched positions touching the floor with the hands on each landing. Then introduce the idea of reaching the hands forward to touch the floor and bringing the feet to meet them with a jump. As the children's confidence grows, suggest they kick their feet backwards high in the air.

**Pigs**

Have the children practise stretching and curling while lying on their backs, then let them experiment with rocking and rolling actions as if they were enjoying the farmyard mud.

**Horses**

Rise up on tiptoe with elbows bent and hands holding imaginary reins. Practise light, rhythmic trotting on the spot with head and knees held high. Contrast this with strong, galloping actions all over the movement space or in one big circle round the room.

The possibilities of Old MacDonald and his farmyard animals are almost limitless. Introduce leaping frogs, swooping birds, darting fish, and maybe even prowling farmyard monsters. If your imagination runs dry, the children will supply you with suggestions of their own.

## CONTRASTING ACTION IDEAS

With children of this age the emphasis of each movement session is on enjoyment, but it is important to encourage variety and contrast in the children's body shapes and actions. Opportunities to do this can be introduced into many of the action ideas outlined in this chapter. For example, Old MacDonald's horse can trot lightly and then gallop strongly; tiptoe statues can be brought to life with alternate strong and light travelling actions. The following contrasting rhymes, introduced in sequence, will serve to accentuate the differences in speed and strength.

**Pitter, patter**

Pitter, patter, pitter, patter,
Listen to the rain,
Pitter, patter, pitter, patter,
On the window pane.

Say the rhyme together while lightly tapping fingertips to the rhythm of the words. Accompany the children's tapping actions with rhythmic tambourine taps, and introduce unexpected stopping points when the children must freeze with wide-stretched fingers. Similarly, introduce and practise running lightly and stopping in statue shapes with arms and fingers stretched high and wide.

**Rain, rain, go away**

Rain, rain, go away,
Come again another day.
Rain, rain, go away,
Come again on washing day.

Clap your hands and, lifting knees high, stamp your feet strongly and rhythmically on the spot to the words of the rhyme. Then introduce the idea of moving backwards on 'go away' and forwards on 'come again'.

## STORIES IN MOVEMENT

When the children can change the speed and strength of their actions and can start and stop on cue, they are ready for other challenging action ideas. You can begin to introduce familiar stories as a stimulus for their movement sessions. The aim is to use stories as a starting point for all sorts of movement activities, not to use movement as a story-telling device. The focus is therefore on the children's interpretations of story characters and not on showing in sequence the events in the story as they occur.

It is important to spend time introducing the story and familiarising the children with the characters and action so that they focus on what they are doing rather than on what happens next. A well planned and prepared story offers marvellous opportunities for creative movement and dance sessions. The following suggestions illustrate what can be achieved.

**The three little pigs**

Practise making piglet shapes and then trotting on tiptoe with knees high and with hands held high in front of the chest. Develop this into a follow-my-leader tiptoe game with you as mother or father pig, inviting the statue-still piglets to join the line by touching them gently one by one. Finish by tiptoeing out of the line one by one and waving goodbye.

The house made of straw

The children jump high and fling arms wide to scatter the straw all over the floor, then bend slowly, scoop up a huge armful of straw, and carry it to the centre of the room. They curl up small without touching each other and then rise slowly together to form a tall, stretched pile of straw. Finally, they spread into a group circle.

| | |
|---|---|
| The big bad wolf | All make wolf shapes on wide-apart legs with high, strong arms and stretched, spiky claws. Play a game in which three or four chosen wolves prowl in and out around the circle and make their way back to their places. |

| | |
|---|---|
| He huffed and he puffed | Choose one wolf to stand in the centre of the circle. Everyone joins in with the puffing and blowing actions as you say the words, and then collapses to the floor as the house is blown down. |
| The house made of sticks | All stand with legs spread wide and hands straight and make strong, repetitive, rhythmic actions to represent chopping. You stand in the centre of the room and ask the children to carry, push, pull, or drag their piles of sticks towards you. Next they should jerk and jolt their fingers, arms, heads, and legs in turn to make sharp shapes, then link a hand, an elbow or a knee with someone nearby to make the shape of a stick house. |
| He huffed and he puffed | You prowl around the children's frozen house shape as the wolf. Ask them to say the words while you blow. The children collapse to the floor, as before. |
| The house made of bricks | Ask the children to stagger with imaginary piles of bricks to spaces around the sides of the room, then place their loads on the floor before they build the wall brick by brick, stretching and reaching further and further as it gets higher. All then join hands to form a strong, safe wall around the house. You take the role of the wolf (or choose one of the children) and creep round the outside of the group circle shape looking for a way in. |
| Happy ever after | Everyone dances round the circle clapping their hands. |

**The hare and the tortoise**

'Wake up tortoise!
Let's see your face!
Come on tortoise,
Let's have a race!'
The race has only just begun
And Hoppity hare is having fun.
Hare is happy,
He stops for a chat;
Then he yawns and takes a nap.
Poor old tortoise,
He can't stand the pace,
Not for him a tiring race.
So slow, slow, very slow,
Ready, steady, tortoise . . . go!

'Wake up tortoise!
Let's see your face!
Come on tortoise,
Let's have a race!'

*Begin curled up small with knees and hands on the floor. Slowly stretch into tortoise shapes on hands and feet with arched backs and stretched necks. Then plod slowly from place to place, finally curling small again.*

The race has only just begun
And Hoppity hare is having fun.

*Make a sudden jump up on to two bent legs with fingertip ears high in the air. Hop or jump on the spot, then from place to place.*

Hare is happy,
He stops for a chat;
Then he yawns and takes a nap.

*A wide, yawning stretch from a frozen hare shape, followed by slowly sinking and shrinking back into a tight, round curled-up shape with hands and knees on the floor.*

Poor old tortoise,
He can't stand the pace,
Not for him a tiring race.

*Slow stretching, arching, and balancing, as before, followed by a sudden, curling action. Introduce the idea of the tortoise stretching its neck to look around before suddenly pulling it back into its arched shell.*

So slow, slow, very slow,
Ready, steady, tortoise . . . go!

*As you say the words of the rhyme, the children plod slowly towards you in the centre of the room.*

# 3 LOOK! LOOK! WHAT I CAN DO!

## MOVEMENT MILESTONES FROM FIVE TO SEVEN YEARS

Typical five year olds are active and energetic. They enjoy all physical activities and delight in the joy of moving. They are assertive, boisterous, and physically confident. All the exuberance, agility, and activity of their pre-school years have prepared them for the movement milestones which lie ahead. They are eager to accept new challenges, master new skills, and explore new images and ideas in action.

Between five and seven, the children's rate of growth steadily decreases. Their bodies and bones begin to change, making them longer, leaner, and stronger. They are now ready to gain the complete mastery of their bodies that will enable them to move with increasing skill, co-ordination, and control. They need daily opportunities in the social atmosphere of school to move in a multitude of physically demanding ways and to have creative movement outlets for their developing imaginations.

It is important to note that there is little difference at this age between the growth rate and muscular skills of girls and boys. All children should be given the same opportunities to pursue at their own level a range of movements which make physical and expressive demands.

The following movement milestones are those we should consider when selecting appropriate action ideas and creative movement activities for five to seven year olds.

**From five to six years** ▷ running skilfully, changing direction, and stopping on cue

▷ moving with increasing agility, flexibility, strength, and co-ordination
▷ tiptoeing slowly and quickly
▷ skipping rhythmically
▷ becoming more skilful at moving in restricted spaces
▷ discovering many new and adventurous ways to move
▷ combining two or more body actions (such as running and turning, running and stretching, falling and rolling)
▷ responding to more subtle action words (such as slither, dart, spring, whirl, float) and translating these into expressive movements
▷ controlling straight and curved movements and moving slowly along straight and curved floor patterns
▷ leading actions with different parts of the body (such as elbows, knees, hands, head)
▷ inventing and exploring imaginative themes
▷ balancing with weight on different parts of the body
▷ creating a variety of body shapes at high and low levels
▷ contributing creatively by putting forward original action ideas

**From six to seven years**

▷ increasing independence and an awareness of self
▷ moving co-operatively with others, sometimes leading and sometimes following the action
▷ accurately judging direction, distance, and height
▷ combining different speeds within a short sequence (such as slowly rising and suddenly shrinking)
▷ moving expressively for longer periods of time
▷ combining contrasting strengths (such as jumping lightly, then strongly)

In order to express themselves and communicate freely and confidently, young children need opportunities to interact in a relaxed, non-competitive atmosphere which will allow them to develop at their individual rates. Emphasis should be on individuals' achievements in relation to their own previous efforts, not in relation to the current achievements of their peers. Competition, before the children's personalities are sufficiently mature, can inhibit participation and destroy confidence.

Our role with children of this age is to provide exciting, challenging action ideas which will help them to master their movements and develop new skills, so that their physical and imaginative achievements become more satisfying to themselves and clearer for others to observe.

Between five and seven, as the children mature and develop, the focus progressively changes from *what* they can do to *how* their actions are performed. At the heart of every creative movement session there should be the quest for quality.

Quality in movement is more easily observed than defined. Some very young children jump with only their shoulders and are quite unaware that their feet have never left the floor. Others bounce up and down with total disregard for rhythm. Contrast these with the child who explodes off the floor and seems to hover in mid-air, or the one whose unwavering, balanced, tiptoe stretch seems to grow onwards and outwards. Such expressive achievements require the child's total mental and physical concentration and involvement. They are satisfying for the performer to achieve and for the observer to watch.

This ideal can be achieved with young children by combining a rich variety of physically demanding challenges which they can meet at their own level with a wide range of imaginative stimuli, colourfully presented, to encourage creativity, involvement, and greater effort. Language has a major role in helping the children to interpret and improve the expressive qualities of their actions.

Each of the following words suggests a specific travelling action. By the age of five, most children are able to respond spontaneously in the appropriate way.

|  |  | *Travelling words* |  |  |
|---|---|---|---|---|
|  |  | stamp |  |  |
|  | step |  | gallop |  |
| trot |  | march |  | tiptoe |
|  | stride |  | crawl |  |
| skip |  | creep |  | walk |
|  | run |  | jump |  |
| scurry |  | slither |  | slide |

Every action can be performed in a number of different ways and we should now be challenging the children constantly to vary the speed, strength, shape, and size of their actions. This is best done by using descriptive words, phrases, and images to which the children can readily relate. These will serve to colour their imaginations and encourage them to greater physical effort and a higher standard of achievement. They will respond with greater vigour, clarity, and enthusiasm if asked to 'leap strongly like an angry toad . . . tiptoe slowly and silently like a stalking leopard . . . walk jerkily and stiffly like a metal robot . . .' This does not mean that the children should imitate toads, cats, and robots, but that they should reflect the quality of their movements.

The expressive quality of many action words is implicit. Each of the following groups of words indicates how the main action should be made — quickly, slowly, suddenly, strongly, lightly, smoothly, and so on.

---

### Turning words

| | | | | | | | |
|---|---|---|---|---|---|---|---|
| | | whirl | | | whip | | |
| | twirl | | spin | | | roll | |
| spiral | | swirl | | curl | | | twist |

---

### Jumping words

| | | | | | |
|---|---|---|---|---|---|
| | | leap | | | |
| | explode | | bounce | | |
| fly | | hop | | | soar |
| | hurl | | shoot | | |

---

### Stopping and balancing words

| | | | | | |
|---|---|---|---|---|---|
| | | freeze | | | |
| | settle | | stop | | |
| hover | | perch | | wobble | |
| | hold | | pause | | |
| stay | | linger | | rest | |

---

### Gesturing words

| | | | | | |
|---|---|---|---|---|---|
| reach | | scatter | | dab | |
| | stretch | | gather | | |
| grab | | touch | | punch | |
| | press | | kick | | |

---

Many other action words can be refined in a similar way. Once the main action is firmly established, young children can begin to make fine distinctions within it. At first the words will need to be qualified with additional phrases: 'swirl round and round slowly and gently, high and low . . . explode suddenly high into the air . . . freeze like a statue made of cold, crisp ice.' Soon, however, the words alone will evoke the appropriate response.

Through constant repetition of a wide variety of action words, the children will gradually build up their own movement vocabularies and come to respond promptly with the appropriate action and quality each word suggests. They will know the difference between creeping and scurrying because they have experienced those words repeatedly in action. Soon the children will be contributing their own words and forming unique action phrases to accompany them.

The rest of this book contains action ideas which will help to extend the expressive movement abilities of under-sevens. All young children are receptive and responsive to the kind of stimuli they provide. Use selected ideas according to the abilities, needs, and interests of your children. Please remember that these ideas are starting points which, once introduced, should be developed in your own way.

Always expect from the children a little more than they seem capable of giving. Isolate for further practice those activities which your observations indicate need to be improved. Aim from the start for movement of the highest quality, and praise and encourage the children's achievements. Observe and comment on what they do, and encourage those with particularly inventive, clear, or expressive shapes or actions to show them to the rest of the group so that everyone is encouraged towards greater achievement. Above all, make the most of the children's physical and creative energy and of their spontaneous enjoyment and enthusiasm.

## ACTION RHYMES

Five to seven year olds are eager to explore a multitude of different ways in which to move. Action rhymes provide one of the many enjoyable ways in which they can do so. They are also invaluable in revealing which basic body skills need further practice and providing opportunities to introduce and develop movement sequences.

The rhymes in this chapter combine several basic body actions. After the actions have been explored and practised separately over several sessions, they can be used to create simple movement sequences. The children will enjoy repeating and revising them over and over again.

**Ready, steady, go!**

Tiptoe slowly toe-to-toe,
Ready, steady, slowly go!
Running quickly, not a sound;
Falling, crumpling to the ground;
Curling tightly like a ball;
Growing upwards straight and tall;
Trotting gently, knees up high;
Jumping! Jumping! Touch the sky!
Hopping now from side to side;
Balance, balance – stretched out wide!
Turning slowly, round and round
Whirling, curling to the ground.

Tiptoe slowly toe-to-toe,
Ready, steady, slowly go!
*Move to a space with big, slow, tiptoe steps, head and knees high.*
Running quickly, not a sound
*Travel hither and thither with fast, light steps and stop suddenly in a statue shape.*
Falling, crumpling to the ground
*Slowly sink to the floor.*
Curling tightly like a ball
*Suddenly contract by tucking elbows, knees, and head into the centre of the body.*
Growing upwards straight and tall
*Slowly unfold and reach upwards on to tiptoe, with high, stretched arms and fingers.*
Trotting gently, knees up high
*Rhythmic trotting with knees high and toes pointed, first on the spot then from place to place.*
Jumping! Jumping! Touch the sky!
*Jump on the spot in high, stretched shapes.*
Hopping now from side to side
*Hop sideways on each foot in turn, with arms outstretched.*
Balance, balance – stretched out wide!
*Balance on each leg in turn in strong, stretched shapes.*
Turning slowly, round and round
*Turn slowly and smoothly on the spot with wide, outstretched arms.*
Whirling, curling to the ground
*Spiral slowly downwards with arms turning lightly and gently.*

**Jumping here, jumping there**

Jumping here, jumping there
Jumping, jumping everywhere!
I can bounce and I can hop!
See me run, and see me stop!
One last jump to finish, so
Leap up high and jump down low.

Jumping here, jumping there
*Bounce quickly and lightly on the spot with feet together. Leap high into spaces with knees bent low on each landing.*
Jumping, jumping everywhere!
*Jump freely in a variety of body shapes (for example, stretched or spiky) and directions (forwards, backwards, sideways).*
I can bounce and I can hop!
*Bounce high, but quietly on the spot in different ways (for example, with feet alternately together and apart). Hop on each foot in turn.*

See me run, and see me stop!
*Dodge and dart with quick, quiet feet, stopping suddenly from time to time in still, statue shapes at high and low levels.*
One last jump to finish, so
Leap up high and jump down low.
*A high or long jump, finishing in a low, crouched shape. Challenge the children to make this their showiest jump of all.*

This rhyme can be adapted to introduce and improve the quality of other actions such as turning.

Turning here,
Turning there,
Turning, turning, everywhere.
I can spin and I can stop,
See me balance, twist and hop!
One last turn to finish, so
Whirl up high and spin down low.

**Look! Look what I can do!**

Look, look what I can do!
I can jump as high as you!
Stretching high and stretching wide,
Can you hop from side to side?
Can you lift your knees and trot
Round and round — and on the spot?
Can you balance?
Well, let's see —
On one leg . . . now on one knee.
Can you skip without a sound
In a circle round and round?
Stop! Stop quickly!
Stretch up tall!
And shrink down slowly,
Shrink down small.
Jump up quickly —
All of you —
And find your favourite thing to do.

Younger children can explore the action ideas in this poem, under your guidance, over a number of movement sessions, responding to each of the challenges and questions in their own ways.

Older children will enjoy working on the poem in pairs, trying to outdo each other in their action responses. Once they are familiar with the poem, they can make their movement sequences unique by substituting the actions in the poem with suggestions of their own after the words 'Can you . . .?' and 'I can . . .'

LOOK! LOOK WHAT I CAN DO!

## CARTOON CAPERS

Familiar cartoon characters can be used to create, practise, and develop a range of contrasting actions and movement qualities.

**Mighty Mouse**

Make mouse shapes, on tiptoe, with elbows tucked in and hands held high in front of the chest. Scurry quietly with high, lifted knees and tiny, tiptoe steps. Display strength by bending arms and squeezing fists tightly.

**Cartoon cat**

Start in low shapes, on hands and feet, then slowly rise upwards on tiptoe with feet placed wide and curled fists held high in front of the chest. Twitch whiskers and lick lips. Unfold each hand suddenly, and stretch fingers. Reach and stretch high, low, and sideways to paw and claw the air with wide, stretched hands. Repeat the clawing action while stepping slowly and silently on tiptoe with feet placed wide. Balance with feet apart, knees bent, and hands stretched wide in front of the chest. Leap and pounce with outstretched arms and legs.

**Cat and mouse**

First divide the group into 'cats' and 'mice'. Make body shapes, as before. Prowl and scurry in and out of each other's statue shapes.

Other contrasting pairs of cartoon characters can be created and practised in the same way. Select from those currently popular on children's television — the children will tell you who or what they are. Allow them to interpret the characters in their own ways as their movement experience develops.

In time, the children will be able to work together in twos, each as a different cartoon character, without losing the clarity of their shapes and actions. Suggest moving and freezing alternately, one behind the other, and moving simultaneously side by side. Children might also face each other and take turns to mirror each other's shapes and actions. Cartoon characters can generate a variety of contrasting movements, and a great deal of fun.

## PARTS OF THE BODY

**H is for . . .**

The way in which we use different parts of the body alters the expressive qualities of our actions. Contrast walking normally and walking with toes turned inwards or outwards. There is a great deal of enjoyment and much to be learned from exploring all the ways individual parts of the body can move.

Ask the children to name all the parts of the body which begin with the letter (or the sound of the letter) H, and then experiment together with moving each part in turn in every possible way. Let the children suggest their own movement ideas first, but be ready to extend the list with suggestions of your own. Stress that all other body parts must stay perfectly still.

HEAD  *nodding up and down; shaking from side to side; turning in circles*

HANDS *clapping; tapping fingers; banging fists; stretching, bending, and joining fingers in a variety of shapes*

HEELS *walking with feet together and apart; balancing on each foot and both feet*

HIPS  *swinging from side to side; turning in circles*

The enjoyment increases when you ask the children to combine some of the actions you have practised, such as walking on heels with hands on hips and head nodding. They will suggest some extraordinary, challenging, and effective combinations.

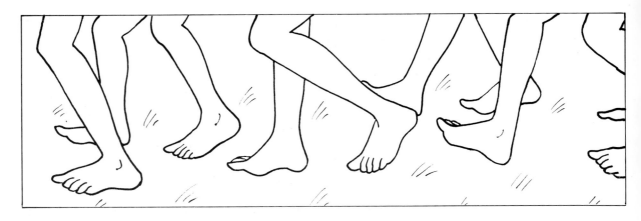

**F is for feet**

Listen, listen to our feet.
Big feet, small feet,
Strong feet, light feet,
Silently creeping, slowly stalking,
Toes are tapping,
Feet are talking.
Soldiers marching up and down,
Funny walking like a clown,
Tightrope walkers in the sky,
Acrobats that leap and fly.
One foot, two feet, three feet, four –
Creeping creatures have some more!
Feet are dancing in a line –
It's crazy caterpillar time!

This poem combines into an enjoyable sequence many different ways in which we can move our feet. It is intended to be developed in sections over several sessions.

Listen, listen to our feet
*Play a strong, slow, rhythmic drumbeat then contrast this with fast, light shaking bells. Ask the children to interpret the changes in speed and strength with spontaneous foot actions on the spot. Add to their enjoyment by unexpectedly changing from one rhythm to the other.*

Big feet, small feet
*Contrast striding with long steps and tiptoeing with tiny, light steps.*

Strong feet, light feet
*Explore and practise a variety of ways of moving feet with the emphasis on contrasts in strength – jumping and bouncing, stamping and tiptoeing, galloping and trotting.*

Silently creeping, slowly stalking
*Move with big, slow, silent steps, up high and down low. Suggest following or being followed and introduce statue stops and balances.*

Toes are tapping,
Feet are talking

*Play a short, repetitive sequence of drumbeats and ask the children to respond with matching step patterns, forwards, backwards, or sideways. Play a question and answer game in which you ask a rhythmic question on the drum and the children answer by tapping their feet to reply. With older children, this game can be developed further in pair work; partners repeat each other's step patterns or take turns to make up questions and answers.*

Soldiers marching up and down

*Practise rhythmic marching with high knees and swinging arms in a follow-my-leader line. Introduce sudden, sharp turns and statue stops. Try dividing the group into two or more lines which march in opposite directions, and in pairs with the children marching side by side or one behind the other.*

Funny walking like a clown

*Let the children explore their own ideas for walking in different ways. Colour their efforts by emphasising the clown's long, flat shoes (which will require high knees, wide-apart feet, or walking with toes in the air or with feet turned inwards or outwards). Introduce a wibbly-wobbly quality by suggesting that the clown sometimes overbalances and almost falls. Finish with a sudden fall, followed by kicking legs high into the air.*

Tightrope walkers in the sky

*Practise slow, careful steps along straight lines with arms outstretched. Introduce occasional stopping and lifting one stretched leg off the floor to balance. Experiment with other balances and body shapes which a tightrope walker might perform.*

Acrobats that leap and fly

*Let the children explore a variety of stretched leaps, turning jumps, rolls, bounces, balances, and so on, and then combine some of their favourite actions to create their own acrobatic sequences.*

One foot, two feet, three feet, four –
Creeping creatures have some more!

*Form a follow-my-leader line in which everyone stands on wide, bent legs and rests his hands gently on the shoulders of the child in front. Step together slowly and silently. This activity can be developed in pairs or small groups with the children experimenting with new and unusual shapes. Encourage them to give their creations names.*

Feet are dancing in a line –
It's crazy caterpillar time!

*Complete the poem by transforming your follow-my-leader line into a crazy caterpillar and standing on wide, bent legs with outstretched arms and fingers. Choose children to lead the line, each of whom dances in a particular way which the followers must copy. This activity can also be developed in pairs or small groups.*

# 4 WHAT SHAPE AND SIZE AM I?

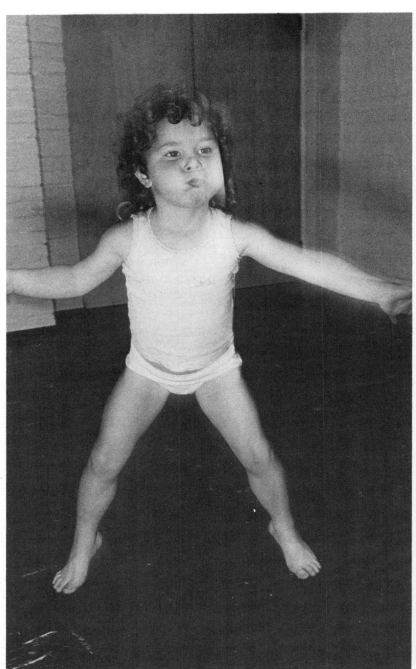

Children become aware of shape and size at a very early age, first by feeling and chewing, then by matching and sorting, later by combining and building. Pre-school children enjoy constructing simple models of their own design, using an assortment of objects, and they have a big enough vocabulary of useful words to describe the contrasting shapes they create.

This conceptual development is paralleled by an increasing awareness of what the body can do and how and where it can move. Even before babies can walk they are learning about their own shape and size by crawling into, clambering over, reaching up to, and squeezing in, round, over, and between all sorts of everyday objects.

When we observe toddlers' body language, the relationship between action and body shapes becomes more obvious. To describe a tall building they will stretch their hands high in the air and reach up on tiptoe.

Young children use their bodies in all manner of inventive ways to describe all sorts of shapes and sizes. Watch them as you blow up a balloon. They will puff out their cheeks, push out their tummies, and use their arms to grow wider and rounder. Suddenly release the air and they will jump, turn, twist, and whirl high and low, this way and that.

When working on body shape ideas you should bear four points in mind. Aim for clarity, so that all parts of the body are contributing to produce the shape. Ask the children to control and balance – freeze – in each shape before they move on. Encourage them to maintain the shape throughout the action when they bring it to life. Point out the children with particularly clear or original shapes so that the others will learn from them.

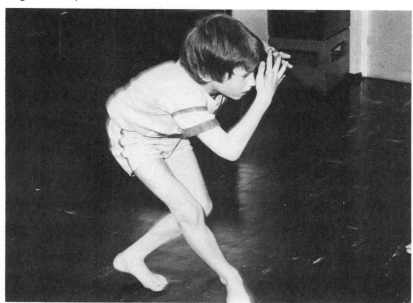

## BALLOON SHAPES
Balloons can be used for an effective demonstration of how shapes change. They can also provide an attractive, enjoyable stimulus for exploring a range of body shapes and actions.

**Round balloon shapes**

Spend some time observing the changes in a round balloon's shape and size as you slowly inflate it. Ask the children to start in curled-up shapes on the floor and to grow a little larger each time you blow, freezing each time you stop. Encourage a clear final body shape on widespread legs with extended, rounded arms, pushed-out tummies, and puffed-out cheeks.

**Bouncing balloons**

Show the children how a balloon bounces high and lands softly and silently, then ask them to practise jumping slowly and lightly on two wide-apart feet, both on the spot and from place to place. Suggest changes of direction – sometimes backwards, sometimes forwards, sometimes sideways.

**Floating balloons**

Describe or demonstrate how, out of doors, the wind makes balloons drift and float, whirl and twirl, high and low through the air. Ask the children to adopt wide balloon shapes and practise turning slowly on the spot, rising and sinking slowly and gently, turning and whirling high and low all round the movement space (without colliding), turning and sinking to the ground, rolling over and over sideways. Encourage the children to maintain the roundness of their body shapes and the light, floating qualities of their actions.

**Twisted balloon shapes**

Practise rising and turning from a low, curled position slowly upwards into a tall, twisted balloon shape and down to the floor again. Let the children create their own twisted shapes, but ensure clarity and quality by emphasising bent legs, twisted arms and trunks, and turned heads. Discuss, demonstrate, and practise appropriate ways for their shapes to travel – spiralling or zig-zagging from place to place, jumping and turning – with emphasis on maintaining body shapes and keeping actions quiet.

**Thin balloon shapes**

Contrast the straightness of a long, thin balloon with the round and twisted shapes explored earlier. Work on rising upwards slowly and smoothly, with fingertips leading, from a low, curled position. Ask the children to look up at their outstretched fingers to help them improve the clarity and quality of their body shapes. Discuss, demonstrate, and practise appropriate travelling actions – high or long jumps, leaping from foot to foot – again stressing the need to maintain body shape and move quietly.

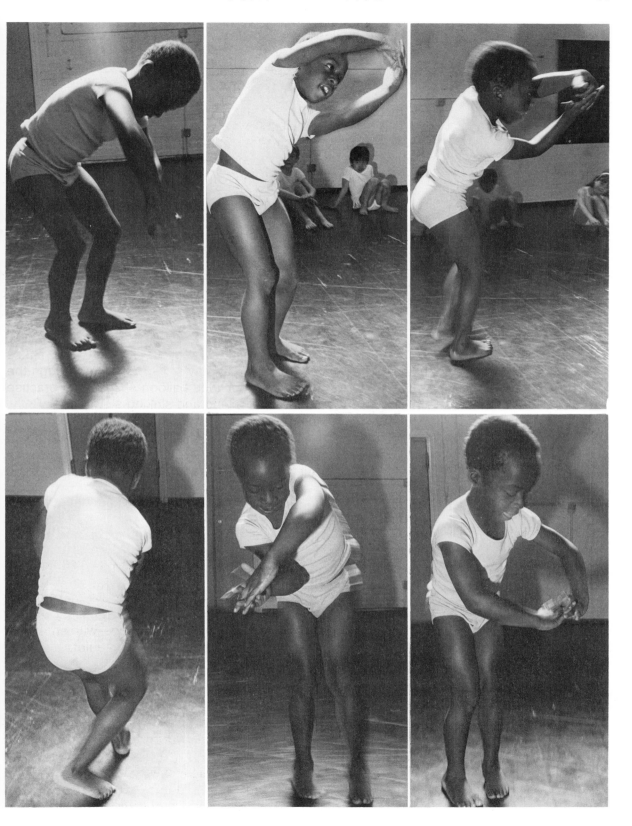

**Releasing the air**

Watch together several times what happens when you suddenly release the air from an inflated balloon. Find words to describe its movements. Ask the children to use only their hands and arms to show how the balloon whizzed, whirled, jumped, leapt, turned, spiralled, and finally fell to the floor. Next, ask them to grow into any balloon shape they choose. Cue them with a clap to move in their own ways when the air is suddenly released.

**Pop!**

Demonstrate what happens when a balloon is burst. Practise a variety of sudden, high, wide, explosive jumps. Then allow the children, starting in curled-up shapes on the floor, to create any balloon shape they wish and to show, in their own ways, how they float gently through the air. When you clap, they must make one enormous jump and land on the floor in a crumpled heap.

These balloon ideas not only give the children opportunities to explore and experiment with how they can use different parts of the body to create strange shapes; they can also help them to realise that shape can suggest how the body moves.

## MORE BODY-SHAPE IDEAS

**Mirror, mirror on the wall**

The children tiptoe round and about. When you bang a drum, they turn sharply to face you. Once they are completely still, say, 'Mirror, mirror on the wall, make me suddenly/slowly shrink down small/grow up tall/fall.' Using variations of these magic words to alter speed and action, you and the children can move into different shapes in all sorts of ways. Later, the framework of this game can be used to inspire the children to grow and shrink quickly and slowly into a whole range of body shapes: 'Mirror, mirror on the wall, make me stretched, sharp, and tall', 'Mirror, mirror on the wall, make me twisty, curved, and small'.

If the children do not know where the 'Mirror, mirror on the wall' phrase comes from, tell them the story of Snow White and the Seven Dwarfs. You can make up dwarfs' names and create appropriate shapes and actions for them. Happy might perform a jolly, hopping dance; Weepy might shuffle along sadly; Clumsy might nearly trip over; Angry might stamp and stomp; Shy might tiptoe with tiny steps forwards and backwards; Sneezy might jump; Sleepy might yawn and stretch and sink slowly to the floor. Then there is the wicked, witch-like queen. When she looks in the mirror she sees a long, scraggy neck; sharp, spiky fingers; bent, bony elbows; and a cross, cruel face. This simple game can be extended over many hours of creative movement.

**Magic mirrors**

Talk about the distorting mirrors sometimes found at fairgrounds which appear to twist and stretch the body into all manner of extraordinary shapes. Then make bizarre shapes of your own which include all parts of the body, including the face, at high and low levels, and ask the children to copy or mirror them. Before long, some of the children will stand confidently in front of the group to form their own magic mirror shapes for their friends to copy. Allow creative freedom but encourage clarity, making sure that each shape is held for a few seconds before the next is assumed. This simple game can also be played in pairs.

**Shadowy shapes**

Take the children outdoors on a sunny day to observe their own shadow shapes as well as those of buildings, trees, and other objects. Play simple games of trying to escape from their own shadows and trying to jump on other children's. Explore the action ideas in this shadowy rhyme and then let the children create new shadowy shapes of their own.

> Shadow, shadow, curled up small,
> I can make you grow up tall.
> Now we're jumping stretched and wide,
> Shadow, shadow at my side.
> Tiptoe slowly; shadow go!
> I can't lose my shadow, though.

Shadow, shadow, curled up small
*Make a tight, round shape on the floor with knees and elbows tucked into the centre of the body.*

I can make you grow up tall
*Grow into a tall, thin shape, with the fingertips leading upwards.*

Now we're jumping stretched and wide
*One sudden jump into a wide body shape, then a number of wide jumps from side to side.*

Shadow, shadow at my side
*Big, slow, controlled steps from side to side.*

Tiptoe slowly; shadow go!
*Slow, light, tiptoe steps forwards, backwards, and sideways.*

I can't lose my shadow, though
*Let the children suggest and practise ways of trying to lose their shadows by sudden jumps, upwards or sideways, or by zigzag running. Introduce sudden statue stops in stretched shapes. Finish by sinking slowly from a stretched shape into a low, curled shape on the floor.*

Once the children are familiar with the words and action of this poem, they will be ready to try it in pairs, standing and moving together side by side.

**Follow-my-leader shadows**

Play follow-my-leader shadows in pairs. The child in front leads his partner with slow, controlled steps, stopping from time to time to make still, balanced shapes, at high and low levels, which the other child must copy. This can also be played as a group game with you or a volunteer leading the line. Introduce other controlled travelling actions such as hopping, jumping, and skipping.

**Ideas from things**

Body shapes can be inspired by objects. A collection of interesting things of different shapes and sizes will greatly extend and develop the children's ideas of what their bodies can do. Such objects can range from things found in the natural world (shells, stones, logs, leaves) to manufactured household items (tools, utensils) and toys (robots, dolls, teddy bears). There is much to learn and enjoy from interpreting these shapes in action.

**Changing shapes**

Early explorations of shape rely on growing and shrinking. As confidence and skill develop, the children can be encouraged to experiment with moving from one shape to the next in increasingly adventurous ways – with a jump, a spin, a leap, a stretch, a fall, a roll. These transition actions are as important as the shapes themselves to the children's creative development.

This verse will inspire stretching, darting, twirling, and spiralling in and out of all sorts of different shapes.

Curl yourself up tight and small
Ready now to grow up tall.
Grow until you're long and thin,
Make your body like a pin,
Or a rocket shooting far
To a spiky pointed star.
Dart and flicker,
Jump up high,
Spiky stars which touch the sky.
Slowly spiral to the ground
Like a screw that's turning round.
Now grow tall or wide or thin,
Find a shape to finish in.

Curl yourself up tight and small
*Shrink slowly and smoothly into curled shapes on the floor.*
Ready now to grow up tall
*Slowly and smoothly uncurl to a kneeling position with the top of the head leading the way.*
Grow until you're long and thin
Make your body like a pin
*Continue to grow until standing tall on tiptoe with back straight and arms at sides.*

Or a rocket shooting far

*Shoot arms suddenly forwards and run from place to place in arrow shapes, with the palms of the hands touching and the arms held straight in front of the body.*

To a spiky pointed star

*Make a series of three, sudden, short, jerky actions to form an irregular star shape, with stretched, flicking fingers, bent elbows and knees.*

Dart and flicker
Jump up high
Spiky stars which touch the sky

*Jump lightly on the spot with spiky fingers, elbows, and knees, shooting and darting stretched fingers high into the air.*

Slowly spiral to the ground
Like a screw that's turning round

*Use a finger to draw high to low spiralling patterns in the air. Spiral slowly and strongly, turning from high and wide to low and curled shapes.*

Now grow tall or wide or thin
Find a shape to finish in.

*Let the children find their own ways of moving into finishing shapes of their choice.*

As well as suggesting how to move, body shapes can suggest direction of travel and what sort of pathway to follow. For example, a jagged, spiky shape might be brought to life by moving in short, zigzagging lines. Before children can incorporate travel patterns into their movement sequences, they must be given opportunities to establish and clarify their ideas of a variety of pathways.

## PATTERNS AND PATHWAYS

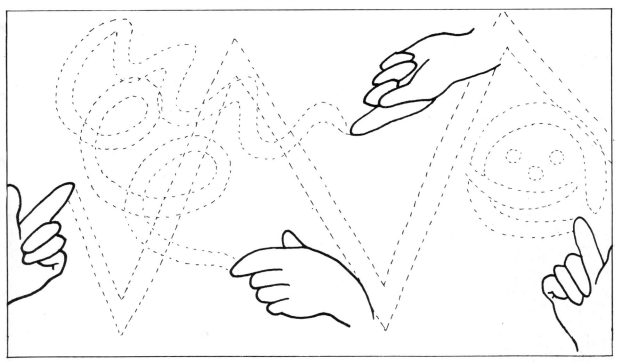

Making patterns in the air is a useful introduction to pathways. Sitting down together, use one finger to draw different pathway patterns in the air. Make all movements large, clear, and slow, reaching and stretching as far as possible high and low and from side to side. Keep the sequences short and change arms frequently to avoid fatigue. Begin with patterns of long, slow, straight lines, then provide a contrast with short, quick, zigzagging lines. Introduce patterns of smooth, curving lines and develop these into large circles, spirals, and figures of eight. Once each air pattern is established, allow the children to interpret it with their whole bodies – bending, stretching, and twisting on the spot and from place to place.

Later encourage the children to create their own patterns and to follow each other in pairs. Suggest drawing letter and number shapes and writing their names in the air. Always seek clarity by encouraging large, exaggerated movements.

As each pattern in the air becomes clearly understood and can be accurately interpreted, play games of follow-my-leader together to teach how corresponding pathways can be traced on the floor. It is essential that the children are already familiar with the game and that they are able to follow and change leaders without confusion (see chapter 2).

## Follow-my-leader pathway ideas

At first, lead the follow-my-leader line yourself with slow, controlled travelling actions until each pathway is clearly established. Later, introduce the travelling actions suggested below, thus creating a link between how to move and where to go.
▷ march in long, straight lines, with a sudden sharp turn to face a new direction each time you come to a wall or barrier
▷ hop in short, zigzagging lines with a change of foot each time you change direction
▷ run in curved, twisting lines, weaving in and out of spaces to trace letters and numbers on the floor
▷ skip in circles and figures of eight
▷ tiptoe along spiralling pathways

## Tightrope walkers

Use chalk to draw long, straight pathways on the ground. Ask the children to tiptoe slowly along these lines as though they are balancing on a tightrope, with sudden turns on the spot before travelling back again. Contrast this balanced, controlled stepping with running between, around, and across the straight lines to form curving, twisting pathways.

## Through the forest

Divide the children into two groups. Ask one group to space out and, from low, curled positions, to grow into a variety of stretched, curved, twisted, and spiky forest plant shapes. The other group weaves slowly in and out of the forest shapes with tiptoe steps. Be sure to change over so that all the children can experience both activities. This game can be adapted into an unusual version of musical statues, in which the two groups alternately freeze and run this way and that around each other's shapes.

## Contrasting pathways

Suggest two contrasting travelling actions and appropriate pathways, such as gliding in long, twisting, curving lines, and jumping in short, zigzagging lines. Make clear, contrasting tambourine rhythms to accompany each travelling action – sustained shaking and short, sharp tapping. The children move along each pathway in the way suggested by the tambourine, suddenly changing action and pathway when the rhythm changes. As their skills develop, let the children choose their own travelling actions and incorporate an increasing variety of pathways into the game.

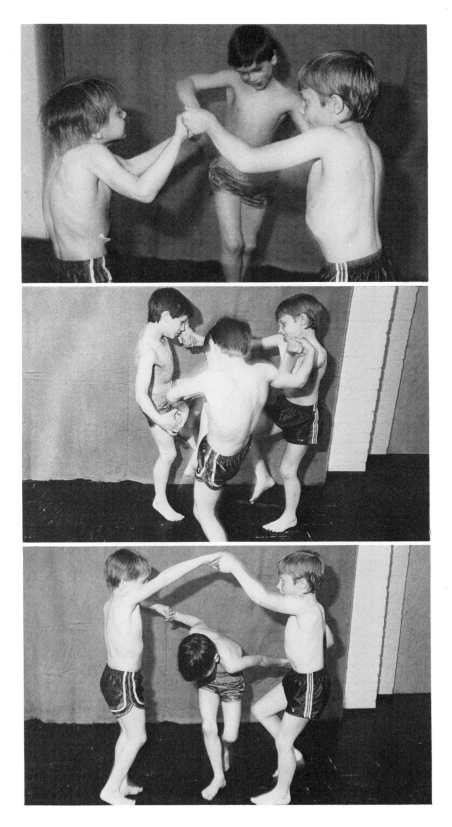

## CIRCLES AND SPIRALS

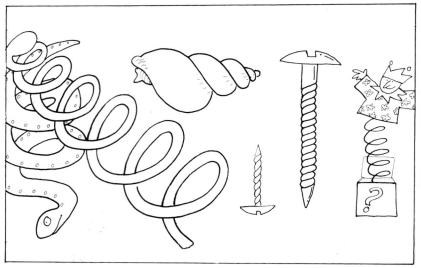

The idea of a spiral is the most difficult of all for children to understand and interpret. Before moving together, show them a spiral you have cut out of paper or examples of other spiral shapes such as a spring, a shell, and a screw. Start the movement sequence standing one behind the other in a circle, with hands resting lightly on the shoulders of the child in front or gently holding his waist. After travelling round and round for a while, lead the children in ever-decreasing circles towards the centre of the movement space. When you get there, tell them to freeze. Let the children take turns to step outside the spiral to look at the shape the group makes.

The spiralling floor pattern can be unwound by everyone turning on the spot to face the opposite way so that the child who was at the end of the line becomes the leader. He leads the follow-my-leader line back into a circle round the edge of the movement space. To start with, lead the unwinding yourself. Soon the children will be spiralling confidently without your leadership, and incorporating spiralling actions in other movement sequences.

As their spatial awareness develops, the children will be able, with practice, to turn their lines into circles without confusion, to move in two simultaneous follow-my-leader lines, and even to organise themselves into two concentric circles which travel in different directions.

Movement opens the door to children's understanding of straight lines, curving lines, spirals, zigzags, and letter and number shapes. What better way is there to discover that a straight line will go on and on until something gets in the way? Or that a circle has no beginning and no end? The ideas in this chapter will allow the children to consolidate these spatial concepts.

## SHAPES IN ACTION

Many nursery rhyme characters demonstrate shapes in action. For example, Humpty Dumpty stretches and grows, rocks and rolls, tips and wobbles, and eventually falls off his wall and cracks into countless tiny, jagged pieces.

Most of the other characters in subsequent chapters offer similar opportunities. Among them are Pinocchio, puppet boy, on page 93, and Metal Monty on page 91.

**There was a crooked man**

Like the other characters, the crooked man and his animals and house are created by exaggerating different parts of the body and are brought to life by appropriate kinds of movements. Such characters offer many opportunities to introduce, revise, and repeat creative work on body shapes in action.

The crooked man

Shoot out spiky fingers, then rise on both feet with bent knees, crooked elbows, spiky fingers, and twisted necks. Practise walking in different crooked ways – for example, on heels, with toes turned inwards or outwards, with knobbly, knocking knees. Encourage the children to find their own crooked ways of walking without losing their bent, crooked, spiky body shapes.

The crooked cat

Stretch out on to hands and feet and form crooked cat shapes by bending elbows and knees and turning toes and fingers inwards. Step slowly and carefully from hand to hand and from foot to foot.

| The crooked mouse | Rise on tiptoe with bent knees and spiky elbows, with hands held high in front of the chest and fingers crooked. Hurry and scurry with high, spiky knees and constant changes of direction along crooked pathways. |
| The crooked house | Start curled up on the floor as a group, but without touching each other. Grow suddenly and sharply in three stages, signalled by claps, into jagged shapes. Freeze and then join an elbow, hand, or knee with someone nearby to form a group shape of the crooked house. |

## AIDS TO EXPLORATION

**Stories**

Ideas about size are often difficult for very young children to grasp. They understand 'big' and 'small', but find 'bigger' and 'smaller' confusing. As well as the balloon ideas on page 54 there are a number of fairy stories which can be used to illustrate and explore these size concepts – the Three Bears, Snow White and the Seven Dwarfs, Alice in Wonderland, Thumbelina. Stories about giants have a particular appeal because young children can easily compare their own smallness with the giant's hugeness.

**Apparatus**

All sorts of new spatial concepts can be introduced and reinforced during an imaginary journey in which the children become explorers moving through forests and jungles, over mountains, beneath oceans, and on distant planets.

Simple, safe apparatus helps to make the situation more real and physically more challenging. Provide hoops and tunnels to climb through, ladders to clamber up, beams to balance across, and mats on which to try all sorts of adventurous rolling and balancing. Too much apparatus introduced at once can confuse and bewilder, so start with simple pieces such as hoops. These can be used in many ways – jumped into, stepped over, climbed through, and tiptoed round.

Apparatus plays a valuable role in every child's explorations of his own shape and size. A climbing frame which is designed to grow with the child and which can be added to in subsequent years is a worthwhile investment for children from three years upwards. Once the children can use the apparatus confidently, their imaginations will transform the stark metal bars of the climbing frame into a fairytale castle or an old haunted house.

**The haunted house**

The children make their way to the house, explore it, and finally escape from it.

Forest pathways

Run quickly and quietly along curved pathways, then take long, slow, stretched steps along a straight, tunnel-like pathway.

Into the house

Slowly step forwards and push an imaginary door with strong hands, shoulders, and back in turn, then with the whole body. Explore the house on tiptoe, with hands stretching and reaching high and sinking and searching low.

Cobwebs

Slowly grow from low, curled shapes into high, wide shapes. Stretch out towards other children to make a group web shape.

Spiders

Stretch on to spidery hands and feet and, keeping that body shape, suddenly scuttle sideways.

Spiral staircase

Creep round and round in small, spiralling circles. Spiral suddenly from a high, wide, stretched shape into a low, curled shape. Then spiral slowly upwards and outwards, back into a high, wide shape.

Long corridors

Run and turn sharply along a series of straight pathways.

A wispy, whirly ghost

Suddenly shrink to the floor. Grow slowly, with fingertips leading, into a tall, thin shape. Curl, twist, whirl, and turn lightly and slowly from place to place, opening and closing arms. Suddenly disappear by spinning and spiralling down to the ground.

Skeletons

Jump up on straight, stretched legs with loose, dangly shoulders, bent elbows, and floppy fingers to imitate a skeleton. Dance isolated parts of the body in turn. Create a jerky, jolting skeleton dance, hopping from foot to foot.

Finding a way out

Explore different ways to step over, slither under, creep round, and squeeze between imaginary objects. Finish with the children taking tiny, tentative, tiptoe steps to form a group around you.

## WHAT AM I?

This riddle was composed by a group of six to seven year olds. Let your children guess what it is and ask them to show you how it would move and dance.

> I'm shiny and smooth,
> I wibble and wobble.
> I shiver and shake
> While you gobble and gobble.
> Yes, you can eat me.
> I'm a . . .?

There are more shape and size riddles on page 131.

# 5 I'VE GOT RHYTHM

From a very early age, children respond to rhythmic sounds and music. They spontaneously clap their hands, shake their rattles, kick their feet, and jog their bodies to all kinds of sounds. To encourage expressive rhythmic actions when they are older, very young babies should be introduced to a variety of contrasting rhythmic sounds. We should sing to them, recite and play action and nursery rhymes, tune in to suitable radio and television programmes, and repeatedly play favourite records and tapes.

Repetitive musical rhythms are only part of the rhythmic movement development of under-sevens. There are also unpredictable, changing rhythms, with contrasts in speed (quick and slow), strength (strong and light), duration (long and short), and flow (continuous and interrupted). The monotonous sound of a dripping tap is an example of a regular, repetitive rhythm. Contrast it with the sound of the wind as it whirls, sweeps, and moans, sometimes fierce, sometimes gentle.

## NATURAL BODY RHYTHMS

The human body has its own inbuilt rhythms and does not always need stimulus from an external sound. Music is not an indispensable part of creative movement and dance work with under-sevens. They will happily and productively explore and create rhythmic body actions without any accompaniment.

The ideas that follow will help the children to structure and vary the rhythmic qualities of their turning, jumping, travelling, stretching, shrinking and so on. Encourage them to experiment with changes in speed, strength, duration, and flow so that they can feel the difference between a series of short, spinning turns and one long, lingering, opening and turning action; between giant strides and fast, turning steps; between short, bouncing jumps and long, extended leaps. Older children can combine these and other contrasting movements to form rhythmic phrases containing two or more body actions.

**Jumping**

Make regular, rhythmic bouncing jumps; long, stretched leaps; sudden explosive jumps. Hop and jump in different body shapes and floor patterns. Watch how animals, insects, and birds jump so that you can get ideas for different qualities of movement.

**Turning**

Use different rhythms, contrasting sudden spinning turns, punctuated with statue stops, and slow, spiralling turns from low to high and back again; strong jumps and turns in wide, stretched shapes and then in tight, closed ones. Encourage the children to observe and interpret the rhythmic movement of things that turn — wheels, balls, clocks, leaves, roundabouts, turntables.

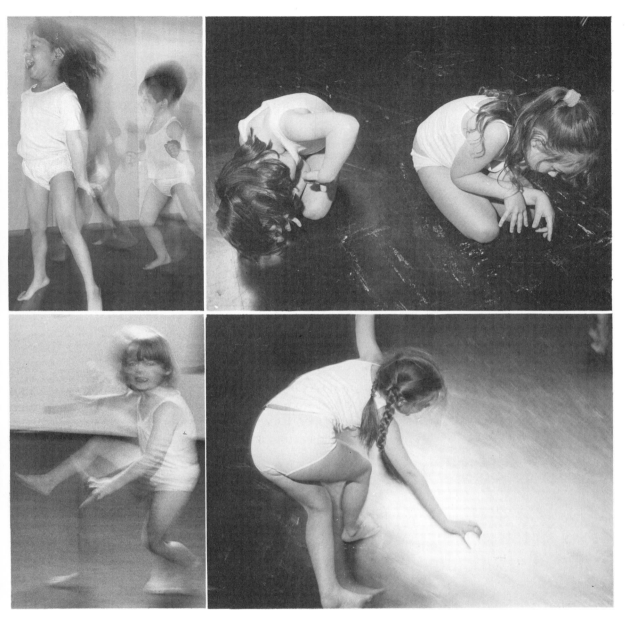

**Travelling**

Contrast giant strides and tiny tiptoe steps; creeping and stamping; trotting and galloping; skipping and marching; crawling and slithering. Listen to the rhythms of different footsteps and interpret them in a variety of travelling actions.

**Growing and shrinking**

Grow quickly and shrink slowly, then grow slowly and shrink quickly. Stretch and turn; jump and shrink. Run while opening the arms out and stretching them. Roll into closed, curled shapes and stretch in different balanced shapes on the floor. Grow jerkily, moving one part of the body at a time. Open out one part of the body, suddenly or slowly, while the rest stays still.

LOOK! LOOK WHAT I CAN DO!

## RHYTHMIC RHYMES

Moving to repetitive rhymes is not easy for under-sevens, many of whom cannot readily distinguish between such rhythms as trotting and galloping, skipping and marching. They need to listen and clap the beat before they can move in time with it.

The following rhymes and those in the first three chapters provide a variety of opportunities for clapping, stepping, skipping, marching, galloping, hopping, and running. Sing, chant, and clap the rhymes frequently. Make sure the children have fully grasped the rhythm and tempo before you ask them to interpret the rhymes with whole-body actions.

**The clock ticks**

The clock ticks,
The clock tocks,
This way,
That way,
And never, never stops.
Tick-tock,
Tick-tock,
Tick-tock . . .

Imitate the clock's regular ticking with actions of the hands, arms, legs, and feet in circular, clockwise motion, then forwards and backwards, and from side to side like a metronome. Introduce robots and clockwork toys to help the children with these actions and with moving in regular stepping patterns.

**Higgledy piggledy pop!**

Higgledy piggledy pop!
The dog has eaten the mop.
The pie's in a hurry,
The cat's in a flurry,
Higgledy piggledy pop!

Small babies can be bounced up and down on your knees to this rhyme. Older children can use it to practise their running, skipping, and jumping.

**Cock-a-doodle-doo**

Cock-a-doodle-doo,
The dame has lost her shoe,
The master's lost his fiddling stick
And doesn't know what to do.
Cock-a-doodle-doo,
Cock-a-doodle-doo.

The children can perform an appropriate action for each line — strutting about as cockerels, hopping with the lady who has lost her shoe, skipping and jumping with the fiddling stick.

**One two, buckle my shoe**

One two, buckle my shoe,
Three four, knock at the door,
Five six, pick up sticks,
Seven eight, lay them straight,
Nine ten, big fat hen.

Practise the actions described in the words or use the rhythm as an accompaniment to marching, stamping, hopping, or jumping.

**Bell horses**

Bell horses, bell horses,
What time of day?
One o'clock, two o'clock,
Three and away.

This rhyme, which can be spoken to a trotting or galloping rhythm, is also suitable for babies who, on the words 'one', 'two', and 'three', should be lifted up – higher each time. Older children can recite it first trotting, then galloping.

**One potato, two potato**

One potato, two potato, three potato, four,
Five potato, six potato, seven potato, more.

This is usually played in a group circle, with each child holding both fists in front of him to be touched, one by one, by the leader's fist. It can also be played as a hopping and jumping game, with the children hopping when they say each number and making a two-footed jump on 'potato'.

**A sailor went to sea**

A sailor went to sea, sea, sea,
To see what he could see, see, see,
And all that he could see, see, see,
Was the bottom of the deep blue sea, sea, sea,

The hornpipe rhythm makes this rhyme suitable for hopping, galloping, pulling, and pushing.

**Tum-tumpty-tum**

Tum-tumpty-tum,
The cat is playing the drum.
Four little mice are shaking the ground,
Dancing merrily round and round.
Tum-tumpty-tum.

Divide the group into circles containing four mice, with one cat in the middle of each circle. The mice start by marching in their circle, while the cat drums in the middle. On the third line the mice start to skip, dance, and clap. At the end of the verse, one mouse joins the cat in the middle of the circle. The verse is repeated, but the number of mice mentioned is reduced by one each time as another child goes to the centre.

LOOK! LOOK WHAT I CAN DO!

## PERCUSSION INSTRUMENTS

You can use percussion instruments both to control the action taking place (see page 21) and to elicit varied rhythmic responses from the children. If you use an instrument unimaginatively it makes a boring, monotonous sound, incapable of inspiring anybody. At its best it gives out an exciting succession of varied rhythmic sounds to stimulate and accompany all sorts of inventive and imaginative movements.

A drum can imitate a dripping tap or a band of marching soldiers. It can beat out a simple, repetitive rhythm or, scratched with the fingernails, it can accompany slow curling and stretching.

It does not take long for even a very young child to learn to dance while playing a hand-held instrument as long as it is light and easy to handle. Percussion instruments suitable for use with under-sevens fall into three categories:

▷ rhythmic, beating sounds: drums, rhythm sticks, woodblocks, hollow skull shapes
▷ melodic, ringing sounds: cymbals and finger cymbals, triangles, chime bars
▷ rattling, shaking sounds: tambourines, bells, maracas, castanets

If you do not have access to any of these, try making your own instruments out of yoghurt pots, plastic bottles, milk bottle tops, tins, and large tin lids. Dried beans and lentils in a box or tin make good shaking noises.

When each child has an instrument, you should instil three basic rules: the children must start moving and playing only when you give the signal; when each has finished, he must stand still and quiet until all the others have finished too; all instruments must be placed on the floor when the children sit down to listen. The last rule will reduce the temptation to touch the instrument when quiet is needed, and will help you to control the children and direct their energies. There is an enormous difference between purposeful dancing and playing and aimless hitting and moving. Percussion works best in a controlled atmosphere where the children have the opportunity to learn from each other.

As confidence and competence increase, the children will be able to dance in pairs and small groups with their instruments. Gradually they will develop the skill to devise short percussion sequences with a leader and a follower, holding a movement conversation in which the first child plays and moves to one sound and the second replies with a contrasting sound and movement.

## Fireworks

The children will soon learn to choose instruments and develop dances by themselves. When they are ready, you might involve them all in a firework sequence. Divide the children into groups and provide them with instruments, making sure that each group includes each of the types of fireworks described below. Give each child the chance to work with each instrument and interpret each firework.

Rocket

To the continuous sound of the cymbal, the child slowly assumes a tall rocket shape. He then jumps about explosively, accompanied by the clash of a cymbal or triangle. Finally, his energy spent, he slowly spirals downwards. If the children are old enough, they can work in groups of three to make a combined rocket. They grow together in one rocket shape, then separate on the explosion and leap about independently.

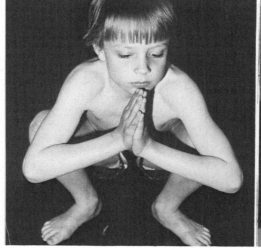

Catherine wheel

The child has maracas, a tambourine, or bells. He makes sudden spins with statue stops, accompanying himself on his instrument and making repeated vowel sounds: O-O-O-O, E-E-E-E.

Jumping jack

Using woodblocks, a drum, or rhythm sticks to make a regular beat, the child jumps, with feet together in all directions.

Sparkler

Handbells make the ideal accompaniment to sparklers. The child uses them to create curved patterns in the air as he makes slow turning and whirling actions. The sparks are represented by sudden, light, spiky jumps.

Bonfire night

For the grand firework display let the children move freely, provided they retain the movement qualities of their fireworks. Ask them to accompany their actions with appropriate vocal sounds and use of their instruments. Choose children whose interpretations are particularly clear and creative to demonstrate their actions to the others.

**Do it yourself**

When you do not want every child to have a percussion instrument in a movement session, the children can still provide a musical accompaniment. Let a small group play percussion instruments while the others move, and change the groups frequently so that everyone has the chance to play.

Begin with short, simple phrases, either worked out in advance or developed with the movement. A good starting point is familiar nursery or action rhymes with a regular beat – 'Jack and Jill' or 'Boys and girls come out to play'. The musicians bang, shake, and tap the rhythms while the dancers skip, turn, and jump. Another idea is for the musicians to play the rhythms of individual children's names while the others stamp or clap. Later you can ask the musicians to play their own sound patterns for the others to interpret in movement.

**Water music**

Water moves in all sorts of ways and makes many different noises. Water words, which you recite to the children, can inspire both music and dancing.

Running tap

Trickling, spluttering, rushing, gushing.
Create a short movement sequence accompanied by a drum and bells or a tambourine. Start with spiky shapes to show a tap dripping, move on to tiptoe steps to represent trickling, then run hither and thither as the water rushes out. Finally stand still – the tap has been turned off.

Drips and drops                 Splishing, sploshing, dripping,
                                dropping, splashing, plopping.
                                Contrast light and heavy dripping water. Use woodblocks and
                                darting actions for the light, staccato drips, a tambour drum to
                                accompany stronger, splashing movements.

Down the plughole               Swirling, spiralling, spinning, shrinking
                                With shaking handbells, swirl and spiral on the spot, then do swift
                                travelling turns, high and low, suddenly spinning into a small
                                shape on the ground. You could use descending notes on the
                                xylophone for this sequence.

Bubbles

Blowing, bouncing, bursting.
To a continuous cymbal sound, grow slowly and lightly into wide, rounded shapes. Jump lightly from place to place, accompanied by light taps on the cymbal. When the cymbal clashes unexpectedly, the bubble bursts with a single high jump, finishing low.

Puddles

Use one finger to draw a big puddle shape on the floor around you; this is accompanied by fingernails scratching the drumskin. Tiptoe round the puddle with long, stretched strides in time to a regular drumbeat. Then, as the drumstick brushes across the drumskin, kick and splash in the water.

Bubbly bathtub monster

The group slowly spreads out into a circle to represent a big bowl of water. To an appropriate rhythm, the children blow bubbles with puffed-out cheeks and tummies, then grow slowly into big, round, bubbly shapes. The monster walks with wide, wobbly steps, then loses his balance and falls to the floor, where he rolls over and over in a round shape. To burst the bubble, you tiptoe among the children touching them in turn. As each bubble is touched, it bursts – making one last high jump and finishing curled up on the floor. The musicians create their own rhythmic interpretation of the bathtub monster.

## RECORDED MUSIC

All those who work with young children are constantly reminded of the inherent relationship between music and movement. When music is used selectively and sensibly, children react spontaneously with increased clarity and creativity. Music for dance is characterised by repetitive rhythms. Rhythmic songs and well chosen pieces of pop, folk, ethnic, and classical music with a regular beat are ideal accompaniments to all sorts of actions. As the children mature, they are able to cope with less predictable pieces of music which contain changes in speed, strength, duration, and flow.

The most successful music for under-sevens is that which has been specifically composed for creative movement and dance. The BBC Education (School Radio) series, *Let's Move!* and *Time to Move* provide a rich source of such music for work with children in this age group.

The following poem can be used on its own or with percussion instruments, but an instrumental accompaniment would extend the children's achievements and enjoyment, and allow them to explore a series of rhythmic changes. You should first concentrate on each movement phrase separately, then work on the transition from one set of activities to the next.

**Time to move**

Time to move into a space,
Slowly now, at tiptoe pace.
Time for skipping round and round,
Lift your knees from off the ground.
Time for stepping giant strides,
Stretching, striding, strong and wide.
Time to shrink and time to grow.
Listen — is it fast or slow?
Time for bouncing here and there,
In and out and everywhere.
Listen to the music play.
It's time to move in your own way.


Time to move into a space
Slowly now, at tiptoe pace
*To a regular beat, the children space themselves out with big, controlled, tiptoe steps.*

Time for skipping round and round
Lift your knees from off the ground
*The children skip round the edge of the movement space with knees lifted high, to a regular rhythm. You should indicate the direction in which they are to travel.*

Time for stepping giant strides
Stretching, striding, strong and wide
*Following pathways that lead them all over the movement space, the children take long, stretched steps to a slow, strong beat. Encourage them to adopt a variety of giant shapes.*

Time to shrink and time to grow
Listen – is it fast or slow?
*From wide, stretched shapes, the children slowly shrink and curl up on the floor. Experiment with contrasting ways of growing and shrinking: shoot up suddenly and slowly spiral down; grow in short, jerky stages with different parts of the body leading. From a final stretched shape, melt and collapse to the floor.*

Time for bouncing here and there
In and out and everywhere
*Play a bouncing beat and ask the children to jump with feet together on the spot, then from side to side and forwards and backwards. Adding high and low jumps, extend the action to travelling jumps.*

Listen to the music play
It's time to move in your own way.
*Provide a rhythmic piece of music and start by simply clapping the beat. Then practise skipping, galloping, turning, and jumping. Check that the children are well spaced out as they dance about the movement space.*

**People at work**

Everyday working actions can be made into rhythmic movements, helped by repetitive music with a strong beat. Encourage the children to develop their actions by exaggerating the movements of people at work. You must stress that they should not merely imitate actions, but make them larger than life, emphasising the rhythm inherent in the movements.

Roadworks use picks, shovels, drills, and hammers; they bend, lift, and carry. Farmworkers dig and plant, cut and stack, scoop and gather.

**Machines**

Use a BBC sound effects record or a tape of machine noises to explore the movement possibilities of different sorts of machines and engines.

Wheels

You might start with different kinds of wheels – steering wheels and car wheels, trains, bicycles, buses. Then find out about the speed, strength, duration, and flow of the movements of spinning machines such as washing machines, tumble driers, and food mixers. Experiment with spinning on two feet with exaggerated arm and leg movements to create rhythmic, spinning, machine wheels. The children can form a circle to whirl and twirl, stop and to together, as one big wheel.

Pistons

Any regular beat can accompany the rising and sinking of pistons. Contrasts can be introduced by making the pistons rise slowly and strongly, then sink suddenly; by starting with slow, strong, rising and sinking actions and gradually increasing the tempo so that actions become shorter and sharper.

Rods

Slow, strong, emphatic rhythmic phrases stimulate the forwards and backwards, pushing and pulling actions of rods. The children could work in pairs, holding both hands, rocking backwards and forwards. Insist on slow, regular, repetitive actions which maintain the same rhythmic phrasing throughout.

Machines in motion

Organise the children into one big circle or several small ones and play music which has no regular rhythmic structure. Encourage the wheels, pistons, rods – and to perform their actions one after the other. Incorporate the working actions in a group where one child starts the action and the others join in one by one until the group forms a single working machine.

## VOICE SOUNDS AND WORD RHYTHMS

Vocal sounds can stimulate and accompany all sorts of expressive actions. Children rely heavily on voice modulation and contrasting vocal sounds to express the speed, strength, duration, and flow of movement. You can exploit this by saying words in different ways. 'Stretch' can sound sudden and sharp, or it can be drawn out to last a long time – 'S-t-rrr-e-tch'.

Words can be used to create continuity or interrupt the flow of movement. They also have inherent qualities. There are slow words – creep, crawl, slither, linger, freeze, melt; quick words – dart, dab, sparkle, flicker, flutter, shiver; light words – glide, float, swivel, whirl, hover; strong words – push, pull, twist, stamp, whip.

The voice can provide a wordless accompaniment, with 'ooh-mm-ssh-ee-whee' providing the stimulus and rhythm for an action sequence. The children will provide a wide variety of voice sounds and nonsense words to go with their movements.

The following poem provides an opportunity for you and the children to experiment with voice sounds and rhythmic words to accompany contrasting movements.

**Stormy weather**

When the wind whirls, curls, and swirls . . . WHOOSH
The leaves fly, fling, and twirl . . . SWOOSH
Spiralling round and down and round . . . SSH
Floating and flying to the ground . . .WHEE
Then thunder cracks and rolls and crashes . . . BOOM
As lightning leaps and darts and flashes . . . CRACK
Raindrops drum upon the ground,
Pitter, patter, bouncing sounds . . . T-T-T
Soon the storm has died away . . . SSSH
It's left a rainbow in its way.

When the wind whirls, curls, and swirls . . . WHOOSH
*Turn from high to low level.*
The leaves fly, fling, and twirl . . .SWOOSH
*Make high, turning, twirling jumps and long, stretched leaps. Pause from time to time when the wind dies down for a moment.*
Spiralling round and down and round . . . SSH
*Turn steadily downwards from wide, stretched shapes to low, curled ones as the voice sinks lower on the words 'round' and 'down'.*
Floating and flying to the ground . . . WHEE
*Rise and leap high, then settle on the ground. Repeat these words to form high and low phrases which are paralleled in movement.*
Then thunder cracks and rolls and crashes . . . BOOM
*Use sudden, staccato voice sounds to accompany sudden opening-out shapes, both on and off the ground. Roll the Rs as you roll your body, then suddenly break out in curled or stretched body shapes.*

As lightning leaps and darts and flashes . . . CRACK

*Make sudden, staccato jumps with pointing fingers, elbows, and knees. Accompany them with clicks made with the fingers or tongue, and loud, sharp hand claps.*

Raindrops drum upon the ground,
Pitter, patter, bouncing sounds . . . T-T-T

*Listen to the feet as they make light, tapping sounds on the spot, then use clicking and clucking voice sounds to accompany bouncing, jumping, and hopping.*

Soon the storm has died away . . . SSH

*Slowly whirl and twirl, high and low. Finally sink to the ground.*

It's left a rainbow in its way.

*Rainbows are arched, wide, and stretched. The children interpret these words in their actions.*

# 6 MOVING INTO MAKE-BELIEVE

In young children, imagination is the key to expressive movement. We must supply them with rich and varied imaginative stimuli to which they can respond creatively in their individual ways. The ideas in this chapter provide excellent stimuli for many contrasting, creative, movement activities. They can be reintroduced and extended over a number of sessions with sustained enjoyment. Many imaginative activities can be stimulated by everyday objects such as hats and shoes.

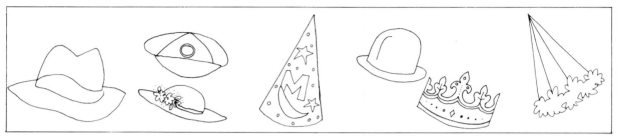

**Whose hat is that?**

Bring to the movement session as many different kinds of headgear as you can find, even if you can manage only an old hat of your own or a crash helmet. Supplement these real hats with pictures of others cut from magazines and pasted on cards. Two or three items are enough for each session.

Begin by asking the children to identify the kind of person who wears each hat, then talk about the everyday actions that person might perform.

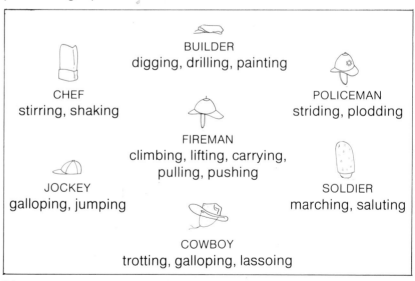

BUILDER
digging, drilling, painting

CHEF
stirring, shaking

POLICEMAN
striding, plodding

FIREMAN
climbing, lifting, carrying,
pulling, pushing

JOCKEY
galloping, jumping

SOLDIER
marching, saluting

COWBOY
trotting, galloping, lassoing

Choose those with obvious associations first, and spend some time exploring the children's movement ideas. Encourage them to start and finish in clear statue shapes ('as if you really are the person wearing the hat') and signal when to start and when to stop. Ask the children to wear each hat in turn and to move to a suitable rhythmic accompaniment.

After their initial explorations, ask the children to exaggerate their actions to achieve clarity and quality. You might say, 'Lift your knees as you gallop and hold tight to the horse's reins.'

Repeat one or two favourites in subsequent sessions and introduce contrasting ideas which allow greater freedom for the children to interpret each character.

KING'S OR QUEEN'S CROWN

GENTLEMAN'S TOP HAT                    LADY'S FASHION HAT

WIZARD'S POINTED HAT

BATTERED TRILBY                    SCHOOLBOY'S CAP

PARTY HAT

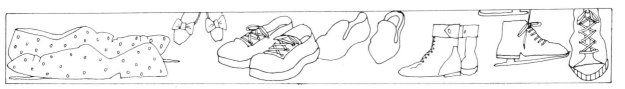

**Whose shoes?**

Introduce, session by session, a selection of boots and shoes, the real thing or pictures, in the way suggested for hats. The children will have great fun creating imaginary characters to wear the shoes and exploring all the different ways in which those characters might move.

HIGH HEELS                    TRAINERS

FLIPPERS                    CLOWN'S BOOTS                    WELLINGTONS

BALLET SHOES                    TAP SHOES

SLIPPERS

## FROM FLOOR TO FLOOR

Young children have such powerful imaginations that they can be inspired to move creatively and with contrasting qualities by the suggestion that the surface beneath their feet has altered. After they have moved freely all over the floor of the movement area, tell them that the surface has changed. Describe what it has become, and watch how the children react spontaneously with appropriate actions:

▷ bouncing, leaping, jumping, on a soft, springy floor
▷ stepping, balancing, falling, on a slippery, slidy floor
▷ running, hopping, on a hot, fiery floor
▷ reaching, stretching, clambering, climbing, over a jagged, rocky floor
▷ stamping, leaping, across a wet, puddly floor
▷ stomping, sinking, pulling, on a sticky, muddy floor

The children will have no difficulty in responding promptly to whatever surface you suggest. Indeed, you will run out of ideas before they run out of appropriate responses.

## MAGIC MOMENTS

Magicians, wizards, and witches are elements of many favourite children's stories and often feature in their imaginative play. They provide excellent stimuli for solo and group movement activities.

**Magicians**

Rise slowly from low, curled shapes to high, wide ones with imaginary cloaks held firmly in the fingers. Turn slowly on the spot in wide shapes. Swoop high and low all over the movement space, opening and closing the arms. Tiptoe from low, closed body shapes to tall, wide ones, then suddenly stretch the fingers wide as if distributing magic dust. Turn and sink slowly from high, wide shapes to low, curled ones.

**Wizards and witches**

Move different parts of the body in isolation to create crooked, irregular shapes. Step silently without losing these shapes. Freeze, then suddenly swoop low, as if gathering ingredients for a magic brew. Skip with high, lifted knees. Rise and sink slowly and smoothly, as if travelling on a broomstick.

**A magic hat**

Instant, magical transformations allow you to isolate and repeat actions which you think require more practice. With the children in a group circle round you, make a great play of putting on the magician's hat. Invent a magic word and an action to accompany it as you turn the children into creatures or characters of your choice. A child who needs to do more jumping can be turned into a frog; one who is not good at balancing can become a tightrope walker. Whatever creature or character you suggest, the child should first make an appropriate statue shape which he holds until you signal him, with another magic word and action, to move. Tell the child if he is to stay on the spot, or indicate the direction in which he should travel.

**A magic brew**

With the children in a wide group circle, explain that they are surrounding a huge, bubbling, black cauldron. Encourage them to suggest ingredients for the brew and throw them into the pot. Stir the magic potion rhythmically together. Take sips, one by one, and suddenly curl up small on the spot to simulate disappearing. Then turn into another character or creature. Ask the children to show you who or what they have become by growing into still shapes, then, when you signal, moving in the appropriate way.

## MR BINMAN

Young children love to combine all sorts of odds and ends to make inventive models. These creations can be the starting points for a series of movement activities.

Mr Binman is a good example. He is made from everyday objects which you bring to the movement session. You start by showing the children how each object moves: the mop head shakes, tin cans threaded on a string clink and clonk, rubber gloves dangle and droop. Then set to work creating Mr Binman in movement. The children turn themselves into him and his rubbish-dump friends in a simple action story.

Mr Binman is a dented dustbin
*Grow from a small, curled shape into a wide, round dustbin shape. Show how a dented dustbin would rock from side to side.*

with floppy, rubbery fingers
*Dangle hands and shake them loosely from side to side.*

and a tangled, stringy, mop head.
*Shake head loosely and vigorously up and down, from side to side, and round and round.*

He has long hose-pipe arms
*Dangle arms and swing them freely from side to side.*

and clinking, clonking tin-can legs.
*Bend knees and knock them together. Walk with knocking knees and turned-in toes. Dance loosely and floppily in a dustbin shape.*

One day a huge, hungry dustcart came along.
*Moving towards the outside of the room into a circle, the children make stretching and spreading movements together.*

It had jagged metal teeth
*Reach suddenly towards the centre of the circle with strong arms and spiky, grasping fingers.*

and it opened its mighty metal jaws looking for things to eat.
*Slowly stretch strong arms and spiky fingers high and wide. Suddenly grab and scoop towards the centre of the body, twisting and turning on the spot with strong, pulling arms and grasping fingers.*

The rusty bedsprings bounced out of its way.
*Jump high in all directions with knees bent low at each landing.*

A pair of old roller skates manage to escape too.
*Make slow, smooth, gliding steps from foot to foot, stretching arms wide and balancing on each foot in turn, then fall.*

So did the broken clock.
*Rhythmic jerking, jolting actions, with arms stretched high and wide.*

The hungry dustcart went away and left the rubbish dump in peace again.
*Invent other rubbish-dump characters like Bedspring Beryl, Tick-tock Ted, and Skating Sheila and make them move in appropriate ways. Finish with Mr Binman and his friends dancing in pairs.*

## METAL MONTY

Explain to the children that Metal Monty is a robot with a square metal head, flashing eyes, tubular arms, and straight, strong metal legs. Ask them to show you what they think he looks like, and then practise moving different parts of the body in turn: open and close fists and blink to demonstrate his flashing lights, turn head mechanically from side to side, jerk elbows away from the body and back again, lift knees and walk on the spot. Then let the children combine these actions and move about the room in a robot-like way.

Once they have a clear image of what Metal Monty looks like and how he moves, introduce an action rhyme about him.

Hello, children! Here I am.
I'm Metal Monty, robot man.
Press this button and you'll see
I'll tell you how to look like me.
Stand up straight and stiff and strong,
Make your arms and legs grow long.
Jerk and jolt from space to space,
Slowly, though – it's not a race.
Work, work, work! That's what I'm for.
I clear your toys from off the floor.
My metal fingers, long and thin,
Grab the toys and scoop them in.
With two long arms that grow and grow
I clean the house from top to toe.
Now my arms move to and fro
As I paint the walls both high and low.
I'm Metal Monty, robot man,
Dancing like an old tin can.

Hello, children! Here I am
I'm Metal Monty, robot man
*Sit in robot shapes with straight backs, raised arms, and bent elbows.
Jerk head from side to side to the rhythm of the words.*
Press this button and you'll see
I'll tell you how to look like me
*Blink and open and close fists to indicate flashing lights, following the
rhythm of the words.*
Stand up straight and stiff and strong
Make your arms and legs grow long
*Jerkily and joltingly rise into a standing robot shape.*
Jerk and jolt from space to space
Slowly, though – it's not a race
*Move freely and rhythmically as a robot.*
Work, work, work! That's what I'm for
I clear your toys from off the floor
*Jerk head from side to side while flashing lights.*
My metal fingers, long and thin
Grab the toys and scoop them in
*Make rhythmic reaching actions with fingers stretched wide, and
sudden scooping actions drawing imaginary objects to the centre of the
body.*
With two long arms that grow and grow
I clean the house from top to toe
*Run rhythmically in a zig-zag pattern with arms outstretched and high,
jerky knees.*
Now my arms move to and fro
As I paint the walls both high and low

*Trace long, straight patterns in the air, up and down and from side to side, keeping in rhythm, with straight, arms and mechanical quality.*

> I'm Metal Monty, robot man
> Dancing like an old tin can.

*Dance about in a robot-like way. Electronic music will inspire the children and help them maintain robot shapes and qualities.*

## PINOCCHIO, PUPPET BOY

Spend some time talking to the children, telling them the Pinocchio story if they do not already know it. Explain that there are different kinds of puppets and establish that Pinocchio is a marionette – a puppet worked by strings.

Make sure that the children have enough room to lie on their backs without getting in anyone's way. Tell them that they are going to be marionettes and that you are the puppet-master who will teach them to walk, run, and dance. First, though, you must check that their strings are working properly.

**Testing strings**

As you pull each invisible string, tell the child to what part of the body it is attached – arms, legs, knees, shoulders, hips, head, tummy, bottom. The child lifts the appropriate part of the body from the floor and lowers it again when you tell him to. Older children will enjoy having two or more strings pulled at once.

**Puppet shapes**

With the head leading, stand up slowly and smoothly into a puppet shape with elbows raised, back straight, legs stiff, feet slightly apart. Jiggle elbows up and down. Lift and lower each leg from the knee. Move other parts of the body in isolation and give the puppet life by twitching the nose, grinning, and moving the eyes from side to side.

**Pinocchio walks**

Take slow, jerky, wobbly steps with knees high, back straight, and elbows raised.

**He runs**

Move quickly and rhythmically all over the movement space, with knees high and elbows raised.

**He dances**

Let the children create their own puppet dances. Encourage clear puppet shapes and rhythmic, jerky actions.

**Puppet soldiers**

Stand straight and tall. March with knees high and arms swinging. Stop from time to time and salute with each arm in turn, according to which string is pulled.

**Rag dolls**

Create loose, floppy shapes and movements in contrast with the stiff, controlled ones made earlier. Do rhythmic dances with long, floppy, swinging arms and shaking heads.

**Glove puppets**

Use your hand to control the children's actions. When you make a fist, they curl up small on the floor. As you slowly uncurl and stretch your fingers, they slowly grow into stretched, wide shapes. Finish by dancing your stretched hand in the air; the children dance with legs wide apart.

**Dancing puppets**

Let the children choose their own puppet characters to dance on the spot. Encourage them to maintain the shapes and qualities of their characters.

**Real live children**

Ask the children to tiptoe towards you in their puppet shapes and then to freeze. Tell them you are going to turn them into real live children again by cutting their strings one by one. As you do so, they collapse to the floor. When all are lying still, ask them to stand up and spread slowly into a group circle. They then hold hands and skip round together in the direction you indicate.

## CINDERELLA

Many fairy tales can be expressed in an enjoyable, creative, physical way by young children. Whatever story is used, it is essential to simplify the action and focus on the characters, which often provide more opportunities for action than the story itself.

This movement version of the Cinderella story concentrates on the ugly sisters, Lady Knobbly and Madam Wobbly. Develop the characters plot over several sessions, but first make sure that the children are familiar with the events of the story.

| | |
|---|---|
| Lady Knobbly | Grow into a long, thin, bony shape; walk in different ways, with spiky elbows and knocking knees. |
| Madam Wobbly | Puff out tummy and cheeks; walk with legs wide apart on flat, floppy feet. Wobble from side to side. |
| Practising dancing | Each ugly sister does a dance appropriate to her shape — a spiky, hopping dance for Lady Knobbly; a more earthbound, floppy dance for Madam Wobbly. |
| Getting ready for the ball | You take the role of an ugly sister and give commands for the children to perform in quick succession: 'Cinders, fetch my hat from that high shelf . . . my gloves from that bottom drawer . . . my wig from the back of that cupboard . . .' As the children fulfil each command, they freeze in their final positions until the next command is given. |
| Cinderella at work | Practise a series of appropriate working actions: rhythmic sweeping backwards and forwards; slow, staggering steps, as if carrying buckets of coal; strong actions of chopping wood; vigorous scrubbing and polishing. Then, working in pairs, the children take turns at being an ugly sister and ordering the other to do a series of working actions. They finish this part of the story by sinking slowly and heavily to the floor, exhausted and ready to sleep. |
| Cats, rats, mice | Practise appropriate shapes and actions for each animal in turn. Cats creep slowly and lazily on hands and feet; rats run lightly with knees high and feet wide apart, spiky fingers held in front of the chest; mice tiptoe quickly this way and that with knees high and |

fists held in front of the chest. Divide the group into cats, rats, and mice to play a chasing game. The children begin in statue shapes, then the cats creep about among the other children and, when you give the signal, pounce towards the nearest rat or mouse. Then the cats freeze while the rate and mice scurry this way and that.

The magic wand

Slowly stretch one finger high in the air and, standing on the spot, slowly trace large, smooth, curving patterns in the air. Develop these into slow, smooth, travelling and turning actions, high and low, from place to place. Then jump high and low in spiky shapes with fingers stabbing the air to suggest touching things and transforming them by magic.

Cinderella's gown

Start in a low, curled, position. Gradually stretch high and wide, turning slowly on the spot.

Mice into horses

Tiptoe in mouse shapes into a follow-my-leader line, then trot lightly and rhythmically round the movement space. Break out of line and weave in and out, with knees high and head up.

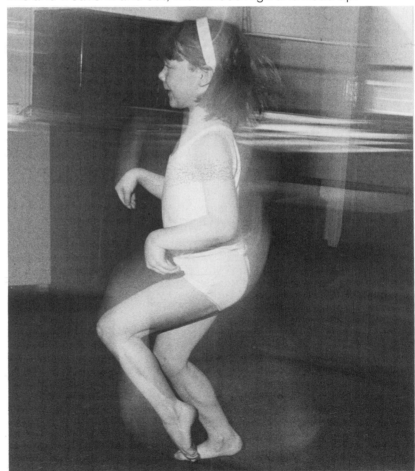

| | |
|---|---|
| The ugly sisters | Dance freely in pairs as Lady Knobbly and Madam Wobbly, first on the spot, then side by side round the movement space. |
| Midnight strikes | Make strong, vertical pulls, as though tolling a bell. Then run hither and thither with quick, light steps, changing to light rhythmic hops to indicate that one shoe has been lost. |
| The prince's procession | March like soldiers with knees high, in a follow-my-leader line, with clear changes of direction and sudden statue stops. |
| Too big | Plod as Madam Wobbly, with big, flat, floppy feet, wide apart. |
| Too small | Tiptoe as Lady Knobbly, overbalancing, then hopping to show that the shoe hurts. |
| Just right | Dance freely as Cinderella or the prince. In pairs, hold both hands and dance round on the spot, then dance around the movement space side by side, holding one hand and waving goodbye with the other. |

## PUTTING ON A SHOW

Simple movement stories can be adapted to form a short entertainment for parents or for other children. However, it is important not to push young children into becoming performers before they are ready. Do not try to persuade reluctant children to take part, but make sure there is something to do for everyone who wants to join in. Do not spend a lot of time on rehearsals and elaborate staging. Productions involving young children should be a development of the work you do in your movement sessions, not material that has been specially prepared.

The following production ideas for the Cinderella story are an example of what might be done. They should be used only after each child has had the opportunity to work on all aspects of the characters and the plot in their movement sessions.

If possible, provide a musical accompaniment, either live or on tape. Prepare a commentary, section by section, to tell the audience what happens next in the story.

Make a large, bottomless box out of cardboard and paint one side to represent a coach. At the beginning of the show, the audience can see only the unpainted side. Place a bench to represent the fireplace.

Select children to take the parts of Cinderella, the ugly sisters, the prince, the fairy godmother with her magic wand, the cat, and the bellringer. The rest are mice, rats, guests at the ball, and soldiers. Arrange the children in groups around the movement space. They perform in the centre of the space, then return to their places until they reappear in the action.

**Preparations for the ball**

Cinderella sits by the fire while Lady Knobbly and Madam Wobbly dance. She helps the ugly sisters dress for the ball and they depart. Cinderella does her work, then the cat, rats, and mice play as she sleeps.

**Transformation scene**

The fairy godmother appears and waves her magic wand to give Cinderella a beautiful gown. The mice are turned into horses. To transform the box into a coach, the rats turn it round so that the audience can see the painted side. The mice take up their positions in front of the box and Cinderella climbs inside. The procession trots round the acting space to indicate the journey to the prince's palace.

**At the palace**

The guests and the ugly sisters dance. Cinderella arrives, climbs out of her coach, and is greeted by the prince. While they are dancing, the bellringer signals that midnight is striking. Cinderella loses a shoe as she runs away.

**Happy every after**

The prince and his soldiers arrive at Cinderella's house. The ugly sisters try on the shoe, then Cinderella puts it on. Everyone joins in the final dance and turns to the audience to make a bow when the music ends.

# 7 DAY BY DAY

Children's efforts and involvement in exploring creative movement ideas should not be pursued in isolation. It is important to link movement with the immediate experiences of everyday life. The world around us is an excellent source of ideas for movement. The words 'I see', 'I do', 'I understand' can be applied to movement as much as to any other aspect of child development. Seasonal events provide occasions to look forward to and prepare for. They can also be incorporated into the children's movement sessions.

## AUTUMN

At the beginning of the school year autumn is approaching. Leaves change colour and fall from the trees. When the wind blows, the leaves fly and float, twirl and swirl through the air. They

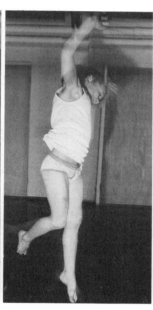

settle to form a crunchy, crinkly carpet where there is much fun to be had jumping and rolling. The children can turn themselves into swirling and finally settling leaves. They can scoop up huge armfuls of imaginary leaves, hold them close to the centre of their bodies, then, with a jump, scatter the leaves far and wide with big, flinging gestures.

The nights draw in, bringing all sorts of shadowy shapes. Hallowe'en is a specially spooky time, with the children making grotesque masks to help turn them into witches who fly on broomsticks, make magic potions, and cast spells. There are more ideas for wizards and witches on page 88.

A week after Hallowe'en comes bonfire night, with parties and firework displays (see chapter 5) and a wealth of inspiration for creative movement.

▷ smoke curling: use hands and arms to make light, curling, whirling shapes all round the body
▷ jumping sparks: make sudden, darting jumps in different directions, with spiky fingers
▷ flickering flames: rise and sink repeatedly on the spot, with flickering fingers
▷ dancing flames: do a spiky, jumping dance all over the movement space
▷ spiralling smoke: make light, spiralling movements, rising and sinking

## The gingerbread man

At bonfire parties there are delicious things to eat — sticky toffee apples, hot potatoes, and gingerbread men. One of the gingerbread men did not want to be eaten, so he jumped out of the oven and ran away.

Rolling the pastry

The children make the shape of a little old lady and roll out the gingerbread on the floor. They stretch from curled, round shapes to long, thin ones, extending their arms, fingers, legs, and toes. Then they roll over and over rhythmically like rolling pins.

Coming to life

You pretend to place on each child two bright, beady, currant eyes, a cherry nose, and an orange-peel mouth. When you clap or give a drumbeat, the children jump up with legs and arms stretched wide and a mischievous expression. Keeping this shape, they run about all over the movement space.

The chase

'Run, run, as fast as you can.
You can't catch me; I'm the gingerbread man.'
The little old lady hobbles about quickly in crooked shapes along zigzag pathways. The mouse rises on tiptoe, elbows bent and hands in front of his chest. He scurries about, stopping from time to time to look for the gingerbread man. The cat, on all fours, creeps slowly and silently from foot to foot and from hand to hand. With you or a child in the shape of the gingerbread man leading, the children form a line of cats, mice, and little old ladies. Keeping the shapes and movement qualities of their characters, they move in a follow-my-leader line.

Fun and games

'Girls and boys come out to play,
The gingerbread man wants to play today.'
The children skip in a follow-my-leader line to form a group circle around you and shrink down into small, curled shapes on the ground. They then grow up slowly into a circle of gingerbread men. You pretend to eat them. You start with their heads, which they nod as you gobble them up; then they drop their arms, and finally their legs collapse and they fall to the ground. When you give a sudden clap or drumbeat, the children jump up into gingerbread man shapes once more and finish by dancing freely and happily around the movement space.

## WINTER

With the cold, wet weather come sparkling frost, stiff icicles, twirling snowflakes, and round, fat snowballs. The children meet Mr Snowman and his friend, Jack Frost.

Snowballs

With strong gestures, scoop snow towards the centre of the body and make it into a round snowball shape which rolls gently and rhythmically backwards and forwards on the ground. The snowballs grow bigger and bigger, and finally the children push them towards you and, from low, curled positions, grow slowly and smoothly to form a group snowball shape.

Mr Snowman

Together, slowly grow big and round, with puffed-out tummy and cheeks. Bring Mr Snowman to life with eyes blinking, nose twitching, and a big, wide grin. Slowly turn round and round on shuffling feet with arms stretched wide.

**Snowflakes**

Big, slow, swirling patterns with arms and legs develop into big, smooth, twirling turns. Encourage the children to look at their hands as they spiral and spin from high to low.

**Jack Frost**

Make short, staccato, jerking movements with stretched fingers, jagged elbows and knees, and light tiptoeing feet. Keeping the spiky quality, add balancing actions on different parts of the body. Develop Jack Frost's spiky movements as he paints all the trees and houses icy white. Hop lightly from foot to foot, balance on one foot, and make sudden, light jumps with fingers darting and dabbing high and low.

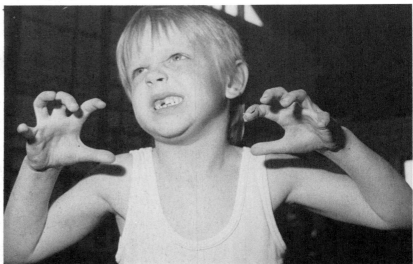

Ice patterns

Stretch slowly from tight, curled-up shapes to wide shapes along the floor. Reach outwards into other jagged, icy shapes, and then curl up again.

Icicles

With fingertips leading, stretch slowly upwards into long, thin, pointed standing shapes. Play a game of tiptoe ice statues with sudden freezes into a variety of icicle and ice-lolly shapes.

Winter fun

Scoop and shape snowballs, then throw them with high jumps and strong, stretched arms. Practise jumping and throwing until the two actions can be performed simultaneously.

A snow party

The children choose to be Mr Snowman or Jack Frost. Keeping the appropriate shapes and movement qualities, they dance about the movement space.

Melting away

Slowly, each part of the body melts in turn. The head nods, the arms droop, the legs buckle, the trunk curls. The children finish in small shapes on the ground.

## SPRING

After the ice and snow have melted, spring comes. Soon pancake day arrives. There are many opportunities for creative movement in the story, 'The runaway pancake' (P Chr Asbjørnsen and Jørgen Moe, translated by Joan Tate, Pelham Books, 1980), on which the following ideas are based. Many are developments of those explored in the story of the gingerbread man.

**The runaway pancake**

The children start as the separate ingredients of the pancake, become the pancake itself, and then all the different animals which try to catch it.

Sifting the flour

Shake from head to toe, with sudden statue stops.

Breaking the egg

Grow into a wide, round egg shape, with puffed-out tummy and cheeks. To represent the egg cracking open, make sharp, jabbing actions with elbows, knees, and fingers.

Stirring and pouring

Stir in big, slow, rhythmic circles, with strong arms and clenched fists. Melt to the floor as the mixture is poured into the pan.

Coming to life

Slowly stretch into a wide, flat, pancake shape on the floor, then curl into a crouch before suddenly jumping up with feet and arms stretched wide. Keeping this shape, run about the movement space on straight legs.

The angry cook

Do a strong, rhythmic, stamping dance with fists held high. The farmyard animals join the chase after the runaway pancake.

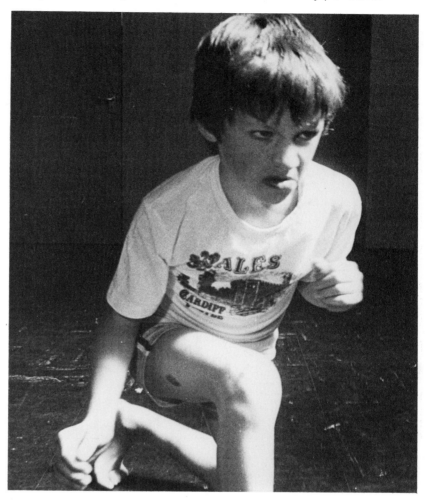

Hens

Hop from foot to foot with flapping, fluttering, bent-elbow wings.

Rooster

Tiptoe quickly and lightly with high, spiky knees, puffed-out cheeks, and wide-spread arms.

Pigs

Grow into a big, round shape with puffed-out tummy and cheeks. With hands held in front of the chest and knees lifted high, the children tiptoe towards you in the centre of the movement space.

An enormous pancake

The children slowly stretch and spread out away from you to form a big group pancake circle.

Eating it up

The circle stays still and stretched as you tiptoe round touching each child to indicate that it is being gobbled up. When a child is touched, he shrinks to the ground.

**Tadpoles and frogs**

As the days lengthen and the weather becomes warmer, the children can be taken out of doors to explore the natural world. The life cycle of the frog provides all sorts of movement possibilities.

The children start clustered together in low, curled, frog-spawn shapes. They slowly stretch along the floor to become tadpoles, wriggling on the spot and then weaving in and out of each other. Gradually the tadpole wriggles its way on to two feet. It grows long, stretched flippers and flapping gills as it flutters and wriggles in and out, high and low, through the water.

Soon the tadpole can leave the water and stand on the ground on two wide-apart bent legs. It holds its elbows high and wide as it puffs out its tummy and its big, bulging cheeks, and starts to jump from place to place. It has become a grown-up frog.

**The ugly duckling**

The ugly duckling is another creature whose appearance and movements change with the seasons. In the winter, after the other creatures have chased him away, he slips and slides on slithery ice and takes shelter from the wind and rain. When spring comes he meets some tadpoles and a friendly frog in the duckpond. Finally, in summer, he changes into a splendid swan.

The eggs hatch

Form a group circle in the shape of a bird's nest. As the eggs hatch, the children unfold from curled positions on the floor. They stretch their necks and push with their elbows until they form duckling shapes with flat, flappy feet, bent elbows, and sticking-out chests and tails. They flap their elbow wings and waddle round in a circle.

Into the water

The circular nest now becomes a duckpond. Two by two, the ducklings waddle across it, each child changing places with the one opposite. They splish and splosh with flat, floppy feet and feathery elbow wings in and out of the circle.

Ugly duckling

Working in pairs, each child takes it in turn to be the ugly duckling. He makes appropriate shapes which the other child copies, as though looking at a reflection in the duckpond. Use follow-my-leader pairs to explore all sorts of funny ways of waddling, with feet turned inwards and outwards. Invent wobbly dances from one flat foot to the other, with bent knees, floppy elbows, and waggly tails.

The cat says 'Go'

Slowly stretch from a curled-up shape to a cat shape on all fours. Creep and prowl about the movement space.

The mouse says 'Go'

Hurry and scurry on tiptoe, hands held in front of the chest. Make sudden stops to look for the ugly duckling.

The rabbit says 'Go'

Make long, strong jumps with legs apart, keeping the knees bent on landing. Gently touch the floor at the end of each bunny-jump.

The angry farmer

The farmer stamps about, punching the air with strong, clenched fists, to chase the ugly duckling out of the farmyard. The children can work in pairs, one as the angry farmer, the other as the flapping duckling.

Cold and wet

As the winter wind blows, the ugly duckling is buffeted about and almost falls over. He shelters from the pouring rain, shivering and wrapping his wings round his body.

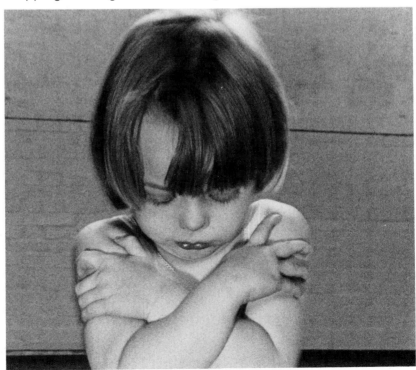

Icy duckpond

Walk in funny, flapping, waddling shapes, with wings stretched wide for balance, on the frozen duckpond. From time to time slip on the ice and nearly fall over.

Tadpoles

With wriggly movements, grow from low, rounded shapes to tall tadpole shapes with fluttering fingers, rising up high and sinking down low.

A friendly frog

Jump with bent knees, sticking-out elbows, spiky fingers, and

puffed-out cheeks. Working in pairs, the children can devise movement conversations between the fat, friendly frog and the funny, flapping duckling. Emphasise that they move one at a time, each responding to the other.

I'm a swan

Starting from a curled-up shape, slowly stretch and grow into a swan shape, on tiptoe, with wide-stretched arms, a puffed-out chest, and an elongated neck. Tiptoe round with arms stretched wide, then sit and fold the arms across the body like wings at rest.

Goodbye, ugly duckling

The children sit together and all point at the swan as it flies away. Finally they skip, waving their hands, in a follow-my-leader line.

**Easter eggs**

To make a family of Easter eggs, start by organising the children in fours, asking them to form group nest circles. Practise growing into an extraordinary egg shape that becomes bigger and bigger.

Eventually the extraordinary egg grows so big that it cracks and breaks into sharp, jagged pieces. This can be represented by staccato, jabbing actions with elbows, knees, and fingers.

When the big egg breaks, out comes the family of Mr and Mrs Egg and their children Master and Miss Egg. Let the children decide which member of the family each will be. Suggest different ways in which each egg character might move — waddling with bent elbows and knees, jumping and bouncing, rolling and balancing, hopping and running, wobbling and wibbling. Allow free interpretation, but stress that all members of the egg family have fat, puffed-out shapes.

## SUMMER

Summer is the time to get out and about with visits to the park, the museum, and the fairground, or further afield to the countryside, the seaside, and the zoo. There are few opportunities for the more ambitious trips, so make the most of television and video to let the children observe how things move. Encourage them to look at the shape, size, strength, and speed of zoo animals, fairground roundabouts, clowns, crabs, fish, and rocks. When the children are capable of observing to a purpose, it is time to move on to a host of new action ideas arising from excursions.

**Getting there**

How are the children going to travel? Investigate all the different ways – on foot, on the bus, in a car, on the train.

Driving the car

The children run quietly all over the movement space, steering to change direction. Introduce the idea of traffic lights for statue stops. At each stop, check the children's stillness and spacing.

Going by train

Form a follow-my-leader line and move with short, shuffling steps and rhythmic train-wheel elbows.

**Out and about**

Include movement in the follow-up work to all visits and outings. The local park is full of people and activities which can be structured and developed imaginatively during movement sessions.

The museum

Even static objects can provide inspiration. A visit to the museum may open up a new world of dinosaurs and skeletons. Start curled up on the floor, with knees and elbows tucked in. Grow with a series of jerky actions, with bony fingers and bent elbows. Stand on stretched legs with dangling arms and floppy fingers. Shake about and clink knees and elbows together. Jolt and jerk all over the movement space. Finally, the skeleton bones collapse in a heap on the floor.

The zoo

Live animals at the zoo can also provide a natural stimulus for movement. After a visit to the zoo, the actions of young children are much more expressive than their words could be as they describe the shape, size, and movement of an animal. They

represent an elephant by dangling one arm loosely in front of their noses; they crane their necks and balance high on tiptoe as they search for words to describe a giraffe.

Before you go to the zoo, spend time giving the children guidance on how to observe each animal. Is it tall or short? Big or small? Is its neck long or short? How long are its legs? What sort of feet does it have?

When you are at the zoo, look at how each animal moves and notice which actions it does best. Does it run, jump, swim, scuttle, slither, dig, climb, fly? Point out that good jumpers have long back legs and climbers often have claws. Runners move on their toes. Swimmers are streamlined and specially adapted for their movement, with webbed feet or flippers. It is best to concentrate on a few animals and look at them in detail rather than wander aimlessly in and out of umpteen animal houses.

At the next movement session the children will be full of ideas for animal actions. You might incorporate them in the story of Noah's Ark or Peter and the Wolf, or simply let the children demonstrate what they saw on their day out.

**Setting out**

Introduce the song 'Going to the zoo' (*Apusskidu: songs for children*, chosen by B Harrop, A & C Black, 1976). Start by clapping the rhythm while sitting down, then clap while skipping all over the movement space. You should point out the children who can skip in time to the music. Next, the children assume the shapes and imitate the movements of the animals they have seen.

Elephants

Extend one arm slowly forwards to form a long, dangling trunk.

Plod about the movement space on flat feet with the back bent, swinging the trunk from side to side. To show an elephant spraying water, stand in a wide, bent shape. Lean forward and curl the trunk arm inwards towards the chin. Then stand up straight and extend the trunk arm high in the air. Sometimes elephants make their own sort of follow-my-leader line. The children can do this in pairs. Each child plods towards a partner, one arm held in front to make a trunk, the other held behind as a tail. The two children stand one behind the other and hold hands to join trunk and tail. They then plod, jog, and dance together.

Penguins

Form a small, squat shape with puffed-out tummy, straight arms, bent wrists, and flat hands. Start by waddling about, then make short, bouncy, flat-footed jumps with flappy hands.

Kangaroos

Make little, light jumps and long, stretched leaps with feet together, knees bent, and hands held under the chin.

Lions

Stride in one follow-my-leader line with heads up and knees lifted high, feet pointed, and arms rhythmically clawing the air. To make the lion roar, rise slowly on tiptoe with the face turned up to the ceiling and the hands held proudly in front of the chest.

Giraffes

Rise high on tiptoe with a long, slender neck and arms stretched forwards to form high front legs. Tiptoe gracefully with head and knees high, walking the arms in the air.

Crocodiles

Stretch both arms straight in front to make strong jaws, with fingers in jagged shapes like teeth. In time to a slow, strong beat, open and close the arms and fingers as if they were crocodile jaws. Walk slowly and rhythmically on wide, bent legs with sharp, snapping jaws. Divide into groups of three to make follow-my-leader crocodile lines. The child in front uses his arms as crocodile jaws; the one in the middle uses his arms to make the crocodile's wide, bent front legs; the child at the back turns his arms into the crocodile's big back legs and wide feet. The crocodile lines weave in and out of each other all over the movement space, then stand still, well spaced out. Finally, choose one child as leader or take this role yourself. The leader starts moving, pausing at each group of three in turn. When he reaches it, the group joins the end of the leader's line and it moves on to the next group. Eventually all the children form one long, moving crocodile.

Children again

Skip all over the movement space, singing and clapping, to finish in a group circle.

All action ideas stimulated by everyday events should be further explored through words, pictures, models, music-making, and numerous other creative, constructive activities. The children can then put their creative movement work in perspective and regard it as a natural part of their lives.

# 8 LET'S HAVE A PARTY

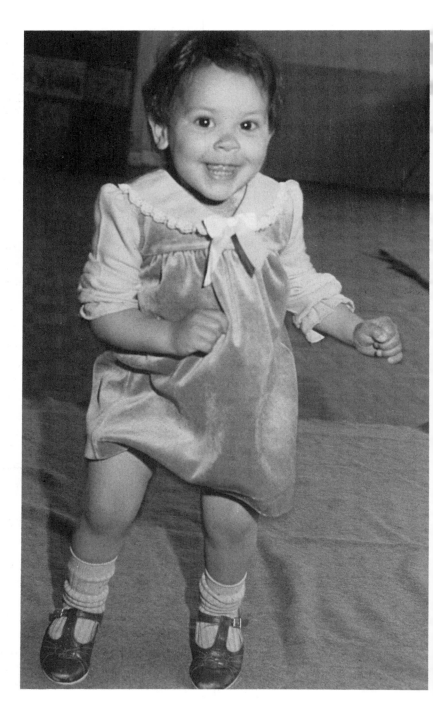

Parties delight and fascinate young children, but they can be an ordeal for the grown-ups in charge. Some people take the easy — but expensive — way out and hire a professional entertainer or take the children out for a treat. This is a pity, as parties and party games can be fun for everyone involved. There are two requirements for success: knowing what to do with different age groups and how to organise controlled movement games.

All the ideas in this chapter have proved their worth time and time again in homes, playgroups, and schools. Many of the action rhymes improve with repetition, and young children love to repeat favourite familiar activities. The ideas can be used in ordinary movement sessions, but they come into their own when one of the children in the group has a birthday.

## SIMPLE CONTROL GAMES

Besides being fun in themselves, control games can provide a respite from more energetic ones, and are useful in preventing children from getting over-excited.

**Musical bumps**

For this you will need music, live or recorded; a tambourine will do. The children space out around the room and you tell them what sort of movement they should make — running, skipping, jumping, hopping. They start moving when the music starts, and when it stops they all bump to the floor. The last child to bump is 'out' and comes and sits by you. One child drops out every time the music stops until only two are left. The one who bumps to the ground first when the music stops for the last time is the winner.

When very young children are playing, none of them need drop out; the game can be played for its own sake, with praise for those who are first to bump down. It can be varied by placing on the floor the same number of mats or cushions as children. Every time the music stops, each child has to bump down on one of the mats. A mat is taken away each time, and the child who does not find a mat on which to bump drops out.

**Musical statues**

This game, a variation of musical bumps, can be played in several different ways.

Animal statues

Ask each child to move in the manner of an animal. When the music starts, elephants plod with trunks dangling in front of them, cats creep, mice scurry, frogs leap, ducks waddle. When the music stops, the children freeze in their animal shapes.

Toy statues

This is played in the same way as animal statues, but the children adopt the shapes and actions of toys — a teddy bear, a rag doll, a bouncy ball, a clockwork soldier, a train, a robot.

LOOK! LOOK WHAT I CAN DO!

**Tiptoe statues**

Arrange the children in a big circle with you in the centre. When you close your eyes, the children tiptoe slowly round. When you open your eyes they must be as still as statues. Children who move when your eyes are open join you in the centre of the circle and try to catch the others out.

**Dancing statues**

The children dance and move in all sorts of different ways before they form their statue shapes. Thus they will turn into skipping statues, turning statues, hopping and balancing statues, and trotting statues.

**Simon says**

With the children spread out facing you, you give them various movement commands prefaced by the words 'Simon says'. They must obey – but only when the words 'Simon says' are used: 'Simon says jump up tall', 'Simon says shrink down small', 'Simon says stretch wide'. You will often catch them out by giving a command – 'Hop on one foot' – without referring to Simon. This game can introduce all sorts of new activities: arms up high, hands on heads, touch your toes, bend your knees, clap your hands, turn around, step sideways – but only when Simon says.

**Grandmother's footsteps**  The children stand at one end of the room and you stand at the other end, facing them, as Grandmother. When Grandmother turns her back the children creep very slowly towards her with the aim of touching her before she hears a footstep. From time to time Grandmother turns to look back at the group, whereupon everyone freezes. Anyone Grandmother sees moving has to go back to the start. The first child to touch Grandmother takes her place.

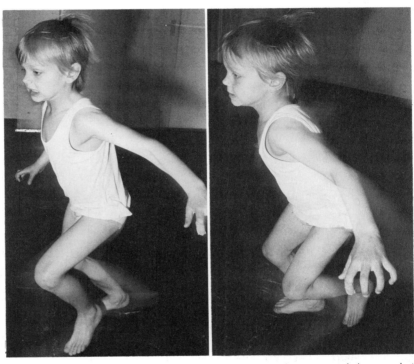

Before you start this game, spend some time practising quiet creeping and stopping and starting. Emphasise that only slow creeping is allowed.

**What's the time, Mr Wolf?**  This is a development of a game introduced on page 26. One child takes the part of Mr Wolf and creeps quietly round the room. The rest of the children follow him, chanting, 'What's the time, Mr Wolf?' He replies with a time – three o'clock, six o'clock, half past two. Each time he speaks, the children freeze and listen carefully, because if Mr Wolf says 'Dinner time', he chases the group back to a pre-arranged point. If a child is caught, he becomes Mr Wolf.

All these simple control games can be played without any winners or losers. It is important to remember that young children do not understand the nature of competitive games, but they enjoy trying to do something better than someone else. Notice what each child does best and try to achieve a balance so that everyone has the chance to perform well.

## ACTION AND SINGING GAMES

The voice as well as the body is used in action and singing games. They often require the children to move in a circle.

**Here we go round the mulberry bush**

Words and music for this song are printed on page 16. During the first four lines the children simply skip in a circle and sing. When they reach the words 'This is the way', they stop and do the appropriate action. All sorts of shapes, sizes, and action ideas can be introduced. You can bring the game to a quiet ending with 'This is the way we tiptoe home', when the children gather round you.

You can add names to the rhyme and ask the child whose name is called to lead the activity — 'This is the way Janet jumps along', 'This is the way Sam steps and strides'. As the children gain confidence you can simply call the name — 'This is the way Bella . . .' — leaving Bella to choose her own action, which the rest of the children copy.

'This is the way' can be used to take the children out of the circle into a follow-my-leader line. When a child's name is called he becomes the leader and starts a new action.

**Name game**

When you want to learn the names of children you do not know, the name game is a great help. One child steps into the centre of the room and, to the rhythm made by his name, claps, stamps, steps, skips, hops, or balances. You could give a clue by matching the first letter of the name with the first letter of the activity — Luke leaps, Suzy skips, Barbara balances.

**Cokey cokey**

Children of five, six, and seven will enjoy 'Cokey cokey', which can be played in a circle.

You put your left foot in, your left foot out,
In, out, in, out, and shake it all about.
*The children do the appropriate actions with their left feet.*
You do the Cokey cokey and you turn around.
*They fold their arms in front of them as they turn on the spot.*
That's what it's all about.
*They stretch their arms sideways to make a big group circle.*
Oh, hokey cokey cokey!
*The children rush to the centre of the circle.*
Oh, hokey cokey cokey!
*They return to the edge of the circle.*
Oh, hokey cokey cokey!
Knees bend, arms stretch, rah, rah, rah!
*They run back to the centre of the circle for the final bend and stretch.*

In subsequent verses the children use different parts of their bodies, specified by you as they return to their wide circle, and end with 'You put your whole self in . . .'

**We all clap hands**

The children stand in a circle or spread out all over the room for this rhythmic action rhyme. The music is printed on page 14.

> We all clap hands together,
> We all clap hands together,
> We all clap hands together,
> As children like to do.

The rhyme develops actions performed on the spot and travelling. The choice of actions is endless: we all stand up together, stamp feet, turn round, march round, shrink small, and so on.

**Punchinello**

The children stand in a circle while the one chosen to be Punchinello skips round inside the circle. As he skips, the children clap and chant:

> Look who comes here, Punchinello little fellow.
> Look who comes here, Punchinello little man.

During the second verse Punchinello performs an action — for example, hopping or bouncing — while the children chant:

> What can you do, Punchinello little fellow?
> What can you do, Punchinello little man?

The children copy his actions as they chant the third verse:

> We'll do it too, Punchinello little fellow.
> We'll do it too, Punchinello little man.

As many children as possible should be given a turn as Punchinello and encouraged to move in all sorts of different ways.

**What shall we do?**

Another variant of these action and reaction rhymes is the movement game, 'What shall we do when we go out to play?' The children step round in a group circle chanting the verse:

> What shall we do when we go out to play,
> Go out to play, go out to play?
> What shall we do when we go out to play
> On a rainy Monday morning?
>
> Stamp and stomp and squelch our feet,
> Squelch our feet, squelch our feet.
> Stamp and stomp and squelch our feet
> On a rainy Monday morning.

In the next verse a specific child is named and a different sort of weather is mentioned:

> What will Mary do when she goes out to play,
> Goes out to play, goes out to play?
> What will Mary do when she goes out to play
> On a sunny Tuesday morning?

She performs an action of her own choice; the other children copy it as they chant:

Mary skips and claps her hands,
Skips and claps, skips and claps.
Mary skips and claps her hands
On a sunny Tuesday morning.

On a fine Wednesday morning another child might march up and down; the children might whirl with the wind on Thursday and freeze like ice statues on Friday. When you run out of days of the week you can start on months of the year, making snowmen in January, digging sandcastles in August, and so on.

**Poor Jenny**

Poor Jenny stands a-weeping,
A-weeping, a-weeping.
Poor Jenny stands a-weeping
All by herself.

*The children form a circle round Jenny, who stands in the centre of the room hanging her head. They hold hands and walk round as they chant the words.*

Stand up and choose your loved one,
Your loved one, your loved one.
Stand up and choose your loved one

*Jenny chooses a partner and takes him to the centre of the circle.*

All by yourself.

*Jenny shakes hands with her partner and joins the circle, leaving her partner in the centre to repeat the game.*

**Ring a ring o' roses**

There are many other circle games, but no party is complete without 'Ring a ring o' roses', with the children all falling down together. Words and music are on page 12.

124

LOOK! LOOK WHAT I CAN DO!

## FOLLOW-MY-LEADER GAMES

**One little elephant**

One little elephant balancing
Step by step on a piece of string
Thought it was such tremendous fun
That he asked another elephant to join in.

*The first child balances with arms spread wide, then chooses another child to balance behind him. The second child chooses a third, and so on until there are, say, seven children in the line.*

Seven little elephants balancing
Step by step on a piece of string
Thought it was such tremendous fun,
But snap went the string and they all fell down.

*The children step carefully along a straight line until the word 'snap', when they wobble about before overbalancing and tumbling to the floor.*

**Nuts in May**

Here we go gathering nuts in May,
Nuts in May, nuts in May.
Here we go gathering nuts in May
On a cold and frosty morning.

*The children stand in two lines, facing each other. During the verse they advance towards each other and then retreat.*

Who will you have for nuts in May . . .

*Line A advances and retreats. Line B stands still.*

We'll have (name) for nuts in May . . .

*Line A stands still. Line B advances and retreats, naming one of line A. The chosen child stands between the lines.*

Who will you send to fetch him away . . .

*Line B stands still. Line A advances and retreats.*

We'll send (name) to fetch him away . . .

*Line A stands still. Line B advances and retreats, naming one of its own number. The chosen child joins the child from Line A.*

The whole sequence is repeated until there are more children between the lines than there are in them. At this point everyone joins in one long follow-my-leader line.

## SIMPLE PROPS

Some party games use props such as hats or handkerchiefs. Here is an example of each.

**Silly old Mulligan**

One child wearing a hat is Mulligan. He stands in the centre of a big group circle. The others walk round slowly, chanting:

Silly old Mulligan
Has lost his hat.
He couldn't find it anywhere.
Fancy that!

At this point Mulligan starts to walk round inside the circle, as the others continue to chant:

> He walked down the street
> And all the people said,
> 'Silly old Mulligan,
> Your hat is on your head!'

On the last line, Mulligan places his hat on the head of the child nearest to him. That child now becomes Mulligan.

**I sent a letter to my love**

> I sent a letter to my love
> And on the way I dropped it.
> One of you has picked it up
> And put it in your pocket.

The children sit on the floor in a ring except for one of them who skips or tiptoes round the outside of the circle. He holds a handkerchief which he drops behind one of the seated children as they chant the verse. That child stands up and moves round the circle in the opposite direction to the first. When the verse ends, both run round the circle in opposite directions in a race to sit down in the empty place. The loser picks up the handkerchief and the game starts again.

### FUNNY FANCY DRESS

Parties are even more fun when the guests are in fancy dress. Some children might like to come as the characters they met in their action games – Mr Binman or the gingerbread man. Any of the games in this book can be adapted to suit clowns, cowboys, mice, monsters, and other characters.

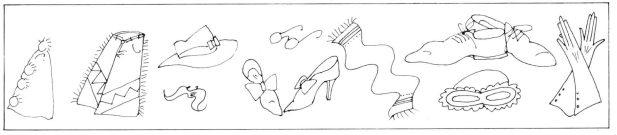

**Clowns**

Tell the children how clowns dress and make up. Explore different ways of clown-like walking, always with the emphasis on long, flat, floppy feet. Walk with toes turned in, out, and up. Balance, wobble, and fall, finishing with the clowns lying on their backs and kicking their feet vigorously in the air.

**Cowboys**

Cowboys stand with their legs wide apart and their hands on their hips. They keep their legs apart as they swagger and stride. They trot and gallop on their horses to round up cattle. They make big circles in the air as they whirl their lassos above their heads.

**Mice**

Mice — and other animals — can have all sorts of different characters and movements. Magnificent Mouse will tiptoe with his chest puffed out and his knees raised so high they almost touch his chin. Muscular Mouse will bend his elbows and squeeze his fists to emphasise his muscles, then swagger about the room. Mrs Busy Mouse will run with quick, tiny steps, and knees raised high.

**Monsters**

The children start curled up on the floor and slowly grow into strange, strong monster shapes. They step and dance rhythmically to a slow, emphatic drumbeat. Encourage the children to demonstrate their moving monsters to the rest of the group, and have them imitate each other in a follow-my-leader line.

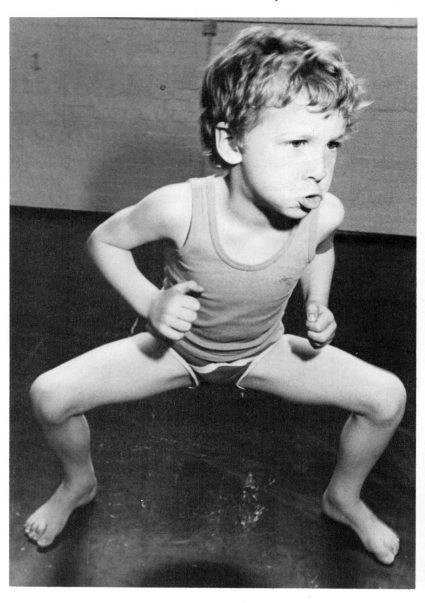

## BIRTHDAYS

For young children, birthdays are very special. Many opportunities for movement are presented by the cake and its candles, balloons and streamers, and party games.

**Birthday cake**

The children tiptoe with big, slow, controlled steps to form a circle, holding hands to encourage good spacing. They let go of hands and stretch up thin and tall, with fingers fluttering high above their heads, to represent the birthday candles. When you blow the candles out, one by one, the children collapse to the floor.

**Balloons**

Using their hands to show how the shape of the balloon changes, the children give three long blows to inflate an imaginary balloon. They then become balloons, using their whole bodies to form balloon shapes, starting curled up and slowly growing round, tall, or twisted. They bounce lightly on two feet and make curling, turning jumps.

You can use real or imaginary balloons to help the children practise jumping, throwing, and catching. Encourage high jumps with raised arms for throwing and low jumps with scooping arms for catching.

**Streamers**

Beginning by spinning on the spot, the children develop this action, using mainly spiralling movements, to whirl and whizz high and low all over the room.

**Party dance**

Ask the children to dance as fancy dress characters or with balloons, streamers, hats, or masks. Encourage rhythmic skipping and turning, with clapping and waving and swaying arms.

## PICNICS

Parties can take many different forms. On a warm summer day you might arrange a picnic party, like the teddy bears. The children might bring their teddies with them. Before you go, familiarise the children with the song and suggest actions to accompany it.

**Teddy bears' picnic**

If you go down in the woods today,
You're sure of a big surprise.
If you go down in the woods today,
You'd better go in disguise.
For every bear that ever there was
Will gather there for certain, because
Today's the day the teddy bears have their picnic.

*The children use rounded teddy bear fists to push upwards and outwards from low, curled shapes to wide, stretched ones. They jump with arms and legs wide apart, then run about on tiptoe or on all fours.*

Picnic time for teddy bears,
The little teddy bears are having a lovely time today.
Watch them, catch them unawares,
And see them picnic on their holiday,
See them gaily gad about,
They love to play and shout,
They never have any cares.

*Clap the beat strongly to reinforce the rhythm as the children skip around freely. With heads high and knees raised, they run, jump, and turn, finishing in a big group circle.*

At six o'clock their mummies and daddies will take them
home to bed,
Because they're tired little teddy bears.

*Tiptoe round the circle touching each child's head, whereupon he sinks slowly to the ground.*

Teddy bear games

In the characters of teddy bears, the children form twos and hold both hands to dance round together on the spot. Then, holding one hand, they skip side by side round the edge of the space.

They play follow-my-leader bears, copying the leading bear's actions and making frequent statue stops. As many children as possible should have a turn as leader.

Performing bears

The children balance with one foot in the air, on one hand and one foot, on hands and knees with one limb raised, and in as many other ways as they can devise. They walk the tightrope by tiptoeing along a straight pathway, stopping to lift one foot and balance. Acrobatic bears jump, leap, roll, and balance. Encourage the children to put these together to form a sequence.

Other teddy bear themes can be developed. The shapes, sizes, and characters of the children's own bears can be used to stimulate action ideas. The story of Goldilocks and the Three Bears could be explored in movement, with Father Bear plodding along, Mother Bear bouncing, and Baby Bear running.

**Tasty treats**

Picnic food can provide a stimulus for movement. Honey might inspire the children to pull sticky hands and feet slowly away from the ground. Jellies offer the chance to shake, wiggle, and wobble in many different body shapes.

CARNIVAL PARADES

If a party celebrates a particular festival or feast day, the children can take part in a carnival parade. This gives scope for many of the characters introduced in this book – skinny, scraggy witches and magicians with swirling cloaks; marvellous mice and scurrying rats; Mr Binman and his rubbish-dump friends. Masks, hats, props, costumes, and face paints will provide further inspiration.

Each carnival character is introduced in turn, and the children explore all the body shapes each character might have and different ways it might move. Encourage the children to respond to each other and develop these interactions into dances. Humpty Dumpty, for example, will grow, stretch, and rock while the king's soldiers march, freeze, and salute in follow-my-leader lines and the king's horses gallop round and round the room. Freeze the action frequently, but keep the emphasis on movement. Other nursery rhymes and fairy tales can be used in a similar way.

Varied rhythms and music are important features of carnivals. Visit a record or tape library and seek out different kinds of music which might be heard during a carnival. In addition to recorded music, equip yourself with simple percussion instruments such as a tambourine, maracas, cymbals, and woodblocks. With music, the carnival becomes a dancing party.

**Brass band**

A carnival parade is often led by a brass band. Have the children sit and clap as they listen to the music, to make them familiar with its strong, regular rhythms.

**Majorettes**

Once the children have grasped the rhythm of the brass band, they can become drum majorettes, marching with knees exaggeratedly high and swinging their arms vigorously. The majorettes march round the room, then weave in and out of each other. Introduce statue stops, salutes, and sudden changes of direction.

**Drums**

Fists drum the rhythm in the air as feet march first on the spot, then in a follow-my-leader line.

**Bugles**

Divide the group into two lines. With arms stretched forward and cheeks puffed out, the children march in lines to the end of the room, then turn and march back.

**Steel band**

Allow free interpretation, but stress movement in and out of spaces and clap the beat to encourage a rhythmic response. Create variety by introducing a shimmering, shaking dance where shoulders roll, hips sway, limbs wriggle. Give each child a shaker (easy to make) or a tambourine. Use the shakers to lead a skipping and turning dance hither and thither, high and low. Finally, dance into a big group circle to introduce the limbo dancers. They arch backwards with legs wide apart and knees bent to make short, bouncing jumps on two feet across the circle.

**Wind band**

Pipers are the musicians here, skipping about fluttering their fingers, playing their pipes high in the air and down by the ground. You can use all the pair, line, and circle formations described earlier in this chapter and in chapter 2.

**Pop group**

Divide the group into four — drums, guitar, keyboard, and vocals — then let them work out their own actions. Maintain control by using the pause button on the tape recorder to freeze the action as if it was a photograph or a fixed frame on a video.

Let the children develop all their musical actions and extend them to include other types of movements such as robotic dancing, disco dancing, body popping, and breakdancing.

### RIDDLES

After the games and the dancing, the children will need to be calmed down before they leave the party. Funny shape riddles are a good way to do this. You say the words and the children provide the solution to the riddle by making the appropriate shape.

I'm slimy and slithery and live in the soil.
I'm long and wriggly and curl up in a coil.
I'm a wiggly, wriggly (worm).

I'm green and slimy, I'm bent and small.
My eyes are bulgy; I can jump up tall.
I'm a funny, fat (frog).

I slither and slide from space to space,
Leaving a trail, at a very slow pace.
I carry my shell-house on my back,
So don't step on me as I might crack.
I'm a slithery, slimy (snail).

I'm ugly and fierce with mad, bulging eyes.
I move very slowly, I'm enormous in size.
Can you guess?
I'm a huge, fierce (monster).

To bring the party to an end, make a follow-my-leader monster together, and all plod out of the room to prepare to go home.

Throughout this book I have tried to provide a simple, structured way of gaining access to the potential for expressive movement innate in all children under seven. All ages and abilities have been covered.

The ideas are derived from what is already familiar in a young child's life. They are an integral, not an isolated part of his development and as such can be introduced, linked, and followed up in many different ways – through words and pictures, numbers and patterns, model and music making. The aim has been to suggest, not to dictate; to provide models which will spark off more and more ideas and thus encourage original action responses from the children. You can choose whether to use the ideas as they are written, or to adapt them to the needs of a particular group.

There is no single way to introduce and teach creative movement and dance to young children. Ideally all the action ideas should be used as starting points which the children explore and experiment with to find new ways of expressing themselves physically. Most of us, grown-ups as well as children, need practical advice and some degree of success before we have the confidence and competence to allow ourselves and others total creative freedom in any art form.

This book contains some of the theory and much of the practice of creative movement. Following the suggestions in chapter 6, you could make more of make-believe by introducing additional props, costumes, stories and characters. The excursions discussed in chapter 7 could include a visit to the seaside with footprints in the sand, Punch and Judy, splashing in the sea, fishes, crabs, rocks, even a sea shanty and sailors and pirates.

Each action idea has possibilities for further development, so look a little longer, search a bit further, and discover much more about the expressive nature of a young child's body. Whatever stimulus or approach you use, make sure that you and the children in your care enjoy yourselves. Enjoyment, after all, is at the heart of learning, especially when you are under seven.

# INDEX

# INDEX II

# INDEX  III